BUNDLE BOOK

Stock Market Investing for Beginners

Discover The Easiest way For Anyone to Retire a Millionaire and Build Passive Income with Only 10 Hours Work or less per year Through The Stock Market

By

Victor Adams

Table of Contents

Before You Start Investing

Well, it is logical to learn to invest before you start some real investment. Maybe a course in investing 101 should be compulsory or mandated. However, here is a story about a very good friend of mine. In the dean's office one of the largest universities in America, he asked if there was a course titled investing 101 or personal investment. He didn't get that answer then. The fact is that someday we would start investing money and it would be a battle between the informed vs. uninformed. There are over 50,000 students throughout a university who have enrolled in Thousands of courses, but you can't find a course talking about investing or investment. I am not canvassing for the change of curriculum I am just stating the fact that what you are going to read here is not going to be taught in universities. Meaning that it would be a long while before this becomes something exposed to everyone.

Before you jump into different financial concepts like asset allocation and strategy, things you already know you should understand the basics: investment characteristics and how to evaluates all other options that are available to you, till you determine what you want and stick to it. You should match your financial wants and needs to the various options and get the best process which suits you and your personal investing goals. There is no single best choice for a financial goal; there are several options you should explore until you get the best. However, what you do is to take your time and consider understanding the basics before you decide to pick one. Whether you are an investor or not, you should understand the basics of investment. Once you've been able to understand those financial concepts you can start investing with confidence. Once you learn how to invest properly, you can reach your financial goals which so much ease. The largest university in the world is the one having no school walls.

Investing comes down to some few basic principles, and without these principles, you shouldn't think or even try to invest. What drives me sometimes is that power to pick the best stock and to buy it. As an investor, you deserve reliable information and instruction so that you can craft out that investment strategy which would fit your need. The first thing is to get that feel for numbers. Research is very subjective, and the analysts offer several options and make estimates for a particular stock. I center all the basics around these eight key fundamental principles; Increasing sales, Expanding Operating Margins, Free Cash Flow, Earnings Growth, Positive Earning Momentum and Return on Equity. All these eight fundamentals would help you discover the best stocks to buy on Wall Street or anywhere. There are several websites where you can get this information and even participate in virtual stock instantly so that you'll know what is perfect for you.

Furthermore, you should also learn to focus on the future. Don't dwell on the past mistakes and you shouldn't get too caught up in the anxious act of checking prices every hour. The long term performance of any stock or investment should be your motivation and concentration. I've had my share of bad days, but I tell you that the bad days cannot be compared with the benefits I have gotten from the good days. The truth is that; what happened in the last market cycle won't necessarily apply to the next so you shouldn't lose sight of the broad market when you are thinking of investing. Furthermore, you should learn to diversify and keep on diversifying. You should have a diversified portfolio as an investor. That is because a diversified portfolio is that mix of dozens of stocks which in several different investment areas yield stronger, steadier and would possess less risk. And in the long run, if some of your investments perform poorly, then your big gainers will neutralize all your losses. Going with the same principle, you should learn to take partial profits in several companies; this means that you should make sure that a single stock never becomes too big for your portfolio. You can sell a portion of your holdings while you keep enough stock to continue to cash in if the ride hasn't ended. More also, you should always sell into strength. The simple principle is buying low and selling high. That is easier said than done right? Well, not really. Well, you should learn to sell something in any position you find yourself and make sure you are able to make a lot of profit from it. So it is advisable that you don't wait too long. Take your chances and make those calculated risk.

You should also expect volatility. You should not be afraid of big market swings especially because they can profit you. Learn how to deal with volatility. This means that you should be able to make money even in the most topsy-turvy market environments. Most of the time I'll advise that you should stick to the 60-30-10 rule which means that 60% of your portfolio must be in the most conservative stocks then 30% should be in the moderately aggressive stocks while 10% should be in the aggressive stocks. What happens when you have this mix? Well, it gives you that smooth path to profits over that long run. The market is volatile, and this mix keeps the portfolio afloat.

This chapter will not be complete if we fail to talk about trusting your gut. The truth is that there is no good investment strategy; things change so you should trust yourself. Don't think that one investing strategy is all wrong just because it doesn't sync well with what the latest guru on Wall Street says or because it is not in line with the weekly report. And who says that you can't create your own strategy? Be open-minded. Open yourself up to those intricacies and create your own principle. That is one of the best ways to grow as an investor.

Debt-The Life Destroyer

Debt is truly a life destroyer. The problem is that it keeps getting bigger and bigger and more people continue to find themselves in that trap every day.It's like the older you get, the bigger it becomes. But why is this happening? Or what is the problem? We find it hard to know how so many individuals can let themselves get into this situation without even knowing it. First, we have to trace the root of the problem. The biggest cause of debt as it stands now is the availability of credit card! But it is a credit card. Yes, definitely. It says credit card, but it is the number one debt accumulator.

The problem is that everywhere you go you see several offers for money, loans and all kinds of cards. This availability is considered the problem. The worst thing is that it becomes very easy to owe multiple sources. You might have a home loan, a car loan, and even some unsecured personal loans. You may have that store of cards, and you'll be wondering when you are going to be able to pay it up.

For the simple fact that it is very easy to get credit card, most individuals misuse this opportunity. They fall into that life of debt from the very beginning and could remain like that for the rest of their lives. But have you ever wondered how? Well, it starts with those free offers you see from retail shops. Then it would encourage you to spend more money than you want to. Furthermore, they make their offers so exciting that you wouldn't want to turn it down. I remember one day when I was offered this bait. I walked into a store, and I was curious. I checked the APR it was so enticing enough. They offered an astounding 39.9%, and they would definitely give you 20% off your first purchase. If you fail to pay it back all at once (which is what they pray for) you'll end up paying them 3 times more!

It is possible to have multiple sources of debt, and it becomes a huge problem when you combine all of it, you have a large and unmanageable level of debt. The truth remains that when you are trying to balance your credit, you find out that you are not making any significant progress because you are only covering your interest charges. Take a look at your credit card statement this month. Is it looking good? Check your monthly payment and check how much interest was added. Are the figures shocking right? Well, that is you and all your bad spending habits on a piece of paper. What's worse is that debt is becoming a way of life, and it is getting ingrained in our culture, and this explains why most people simply accept all terms and conditions given, maybe because they assume that the contract is 'right' and they can actually control it. However, that is not the case. Most people don't even know what APR they are paying on their credit cards. All this information shouldn't be strange to you as an investor.

These persons fail to understand the significance of each step they make. When you get a credit card, you are essentially signing that contact or that legal commitment of earning and paying that set amount each month. Note that it is not savings. It would be fine if you are able to keep to this commitment, but problems would occur which would stretch you, and in this situation, you would be expected to pay up as your interest rate begin to rise. The bigger problem would be that sudden issues like unemployment would cause legal issues because of the first mistake of putting down your signature during your disposition.

Debt creeps on you all of a sudden. First, we are happily going about our daily lives, not paying too much attention to our spending. Then we just pop it on the credit card. After all, it is just some few dollars.

The car needs servicing, the kids want new trainers, and the list keeps going on forever.

But that is not a problem until when one day it dawns on you, and you'll be like; what? When did I spend this much? How did I arrive at this balance? You are surprised at first when you apply for additional cards. Then you start the cycle once more with more available credit. Then that quick check of all your balances at the back of the envelope. Boom, you're surprised once more.

Then you would discover that you can't even meet up with the minimum payments on time. What's next? You apply for a personal loan to consolidate all the credit and store card balances into that easy and affordable monthly payment just the way they tell you. You have just succeeded in robbing Peter to Paul. The only problem here is that you are not robbing, but you are borrowing. Well, you think everything is fine, and you have nothing to worry about right? That is just a façade they want you to believe.

It only comes crashing down, and the minimum payment would become something you can't meet up to again. Then you scream for help! And you start to get financial advice from the experts. Well, Bankruptcy is the last resort not the end of the world, it allows you to start again with that clean state although obtaining future credit after this initial discharge would become very difficult.

Now, this leads us to the question of the century: can we live a debt-free life? It is like asking if someone can survive without a credit card because it is becoming a necessity gradually. My answer is simple. You can live a debt-free life. Yes, it is possible. This is not something from the abstract world or a statement to motivate you; I would back it up with facts. Because it wouldn't flow well to tell you the dangers of something without providing steps on how to eliminate or stop its negative effects.

Let me arouse your interest. Do you know that an individual can possibly save up to $1,000,000 and eliminate all debt they can pay off their mortgage by investing in that safe mutual funds? Credit isn't expected to be all good. In fact, credits are not in the creditor's best interest. However, you can make use of that magic input. The magic input is the amount that you set aside to pay extra bills in that specific sequence. There are sites which can help you do this or you can do this manually, and you'll get tremendous results.

- First, you will go to your last six to seven months of check register then you would list items which you hope to reduce. Note that bills shouldn't be inclusive because they would soon be paid off, taxes, etc. are facts of life.
- Make sure you categorize each entry into several segments. Like groceries, lunches, savings, entertainment, etc.

- Sit down and think of ideas on how you can save on all these items you've listed making sure that you arrive at a 10% total gross. For example, if an item costs $90 you should devise a means of making it cost $80 or even less. But don't forget that it is temporary so you don't need to start so big.

After you have been able to do this successfully what is next for you is to start the Payoff Sequence. The payoff sequence is quite complex but not difficult when you follow the right principles.

1. Make sure you divide the total payoff amount by the monthly payment. Make sure you pick that numeric sequence which starts with 1 for that lowest division.
2. For every month the normal monthly payment to each debt should be made. You should repeat this process until the debt is fully paid.

3. You should pay the minimum monthly bills except the debt two. What this means is that you pick each debt one after the other for each month. You don't just pay little by scattering your little resources around, it wouldn't have any value, and the interest would continue to add up.

4. One thing I am sure this method would teach you is how to control spending, and it would also make you realize that you are spending your money on some useless items and you would need to change that.

The major concept here is to pay off the interest of your small debts first before you use the money as leverage to pay up the rest. First,you face the initial concept of picking your debt or debt selection, and you should agree to pay the one with the biggest interest first. Employing this method shows that you are ready to get out of debt and you are ready to do it quick.

Well, most of the time there are three questions that come to the minds of those who find themselves in debt. First is how did I get here? Why is this happening to me? And how am I going out of this? A pile of debt can bring so much onerous burden. It can also bring a great number of psychological problems also. However, if you take the right step, you would be able to avoid it. Quickly, I would share some steps;

First, you should question every buying. You should ask yourself a number of question about every purchase you are about to make. Do you actually need that item or it is just a want? If you put off the purchase for a while would it affect you negatively? You shouldn't be battling against debt while you continue to accommodate its problem. Sometimes asking these questions would break some bad spending habits. Next, you should keep a fixed amount which you plan to spend on expenses each week. If you plan on buying something which would make you exceed that fixed amount, you should cancel that plan. You should make it of great necessity to give precedence to your expenditure. It should be what you need and not what you want. Furthermore, it is not bad if you go 'low-priced' there is nothing bad in telling yourself that; I can't afford this. You shouldn't carry along that mentality of letting me get it even though I would suffer for it. You should go low-priced and even get non-branded equivalents instead of the items which are very expensive but popular. Shop around for the best prices; this would help you to lower your cost drastically. And when you lower your cost, you'll be able to save money.

Conclusively, you should have a spending plan and stick to it. I know this can be very hard. Fighting that urge to buy something that you really like or because you cannot just get something that you love because you are on a budget. But I tell you that a comfortable life free of debt is better than an extravagant life sinking in the ocean of debt. After paying all your bills and buying the necessity which you need personally or in your household do you have some money left? That spending plan would help you get the right answer to that. The spending plan is just a simple word for the budget. Don't get confused. Remember that the first thing for you to do is to prioritize your needs, create that spending strategy and adjust your finances to the best of your interest. If you fail to do that by ignoring your spending decision and not keeping to the fixed amount that you are to spend per week, it leads to overspending immediately which can lead you into that life of debt. Poor planning or having no plan at all is another factor which can lead to financial problems like debt. Debt is a life destroyer, don't allow it destroy you.

Avoiding Bad Credit

It is important that we should know the causes of bad credit as credit can be a tricky thing. A quick list of what we are going to discuss in this chapter includes; paying late or not at all, maxing out your card, closing credit accounts, etc.

Having said that, below is a comprehensive list of the cause of bad credit in no particular order:

Missing Payments: We don't need a credit expert to tell us that missing payments is a bad thing for your credit history, credit score and overall, your finances. You should know by now credit scores look at your credit history to see how you have been able to manage your current and past credit obligations in order to predict how likely it's going to be for you to miss payments in the future. When you miss payments, you predict the future that you are going to miss more and more payments. It's like your past and even your present, form your future. There are several ways missing payments could severely damage your credit score some of them are;

- How frequently you pay late: For someone who misses payments very frequently, he/she would be penalized more severely than someone who misses payments infrequently. The trick is this; even if you want to miss payments, something you shouldn't don't make it too often.

- How serious are your late payments: You may be *fashionably late* or *completely late*. The difference between both has to do with the time duration. You should know that the severity of your late payment plays a trivial part in your credit score and contributes to your credit history as well. For someone who missed a payment by only a few weeks and brought his/her payment up to date is likely to have a score better than someone whose payment is 90 days overdue or worse. When you have late payments make sure you do all you can to bring them up to date as soon as possible, it's for your own good.

- How current is your late payment: We are aware that the scoring models are designed to forecast how you will pay your bills in future if you keep paying late your credit score depreciates drastically too. For someone having his late payments more often in the last two years would definitely missa payment in the next two years than an individual having no late payments.

Closing Credit Card Accounts: Closing credit card is as bad as missing payments or even worse, you may be wondering how this is possible. But let me tell you that closing credit card account doesn't boost your credit scores; it does the opposite. Closing your credit card account is the most common piece of misguided counsel an individual would receive when he/she asks how the credit score can be increased. Many have fallen victim of this wrong advice, and I would give you some reasons why closing credit cards accounts wouldn't increase your credit score.

First, a closed account will definitely reflect on your credit report earlier than opening a new one. Coupled with that, credit reporting agencies, banks, and lenders would have to follow specific rules which depend on how long the new information would remain on your credit report. Most times, negative credit information would stain your credit report or remain in your credit files for seven years from the date the first debt became neglected. While positive credit information can remain indefinitely, on the other hand, closed accounts in good standing are most times removed from the credit report within ten years after closing! Surprised? That's not all. As soon as the credit score starts deriving its value from the progressive history which is related to an account but the owner decides to close the account, the good report is gone-totally removed from the report when that account is removed. The "good history" of how you had been faithful for years with your credit is gone in an instant, and sadly such history would remain untraceable once you close the credit card account. Yeah, you may be thinking is this really bad? A credit score favors a long credit history, isn't it? Because the length of my credit history accounts for 15% of a FICO score right? You should know that individuals with a fresh or young credit card history are usually seen as more risky borrowers than those who have credit for many years. You should hang onto those old accounts if you can by making sure they remain open. Make sure you do all you can to keep them open, closing them may look very simple and easy, but its negative footprints may be hard to leave your credit record. That is why you need to think twice before you open any credit account.

Another thing closing credit card account does to you is that it hurts your "utilization" measurements. In the short run, this is considerably more important than your closed accounts diminishing from your credit reports. Revolving utilization is a terminology used to refer to the revolving credit card limits that are in use on your credit card. It is called revolving because it changes all the time. For example, if you have an open credit account having $3000 as your credit limit and a $1500 balance, you are 50% "utilized" on that particular account, obviously because you are using half of your credit limit. This particular scaling makes up to 30% of your credit score. And has the same importance as making your payments on time on your credit score. As this particular percentage increases, your credit score also decreases. You must have noticed that the issue of credit is not as simple as you think it is, there is no need to worry so long you understand the simple rudiments which are in this book. Having given you a little detail about "utilization measurements," we would need to further our knowledge

Over-Utilization of Available Credit Card Limits: Just as we have mentioned that high balances on your credit cards increase the chances of your credit score going low, over-utilization can become a big problem. Now I know what you might be thinking, why do I have a limit of $3000 when I can't use up to that amount? From now on, I want you to look at your limit, not as a "limit" per se but a gauge. A place you should never reach. If by chance you happen to be in this position over utilizing your available credit card limits, your best bet would be to use your cards scarcely or in moderation. You should try your best to reduce that percentage as much as possible, and then your score would gradually work its way back up. It is safe to say that the lower the percentage, the better it becomes as there is no special target to shoot at. It all depends on you. I would like you to take this as a rule: you should not reach your credit card limit. Restrain yourself from excessive buying.

Settling with your lender or credit company on past due to account: settling is when your credit industry or lender accepts an amount which is less than the actual amount you owe on an account. Take, for example, you owe a credit card company $15,00, but some "unforeseen" circumstances couldn't allow you to pay that amount in full, a deal for less than that full amount would be made. Once that deal is accepted by both parties then we can say a "settling" exists. This sounds like a good idea isn't it? You are not to pay the full amount, what a relief. Nonetheless, the lender will account for that remaining amount to the credit bureau as a negative item. The outstanding amount is called the "deficiency balance." This deficiency balance is seen as a negative scoring model just as the credit bureaus see severe late payments. A smart option exists for you here; if you can make it possible to arrange a deal with your lender so that he wouldn't report the deficiency balance. If you can come to an agreement then what is left is that you should find a way to pay in full or you may face the consequences for 7 years.

Excessively Shopping for Credit: shopping for credit here means; filling out several credit application. Let me tell you what happens. Filling out a credit application means that you are giving the lender license to access your credit reports. After accessing your credit reports, automatically they post an "inquiry." This inquiry is a history profile or note of who pulled your credit report and the date also. The federal law states that the inquiry remains on the report for the period of 24 months. Nevertheless, credit scores only look at inquiries which are less than a year old. These inquiries are utilized by credit scoring models in order to determine whether or not an individual is shopping for credit or not. These inquiries are utilized by credit scoring models to decide whether or not someone is shopping for credit. It remains the fact that consumers or individuals with more inquiries attract higher credit risk than those with fewer inquiries. These means that the more you make queries and investigations about your credit the more points you lose. Isn't that ridiculous?.Excessively shopping for credit doesn't only attract the attention of lenders to produce inquiries it reduces your credit scores, damages your history and could also destroy your financial life if you're not cautious enough.

Having the thought that all credit scores are the same: We would discuss more of this when we are talking about Credit score in the next chapter. However, we need to understand little for now. Nothing should make us think that all credit scores are the same. This is one mistake individuals make, and it also gets confusing. There are different types of credit score just as there are different types of soft drinks. We shouldn't take one kind of credit score like the other just as we can't take 7up as Coca-Cola. There are several places where consumers could purchase credit reports and credit scores, but not all scores sold are similar. Coming upon this nugget of information may sound normal or easy to you making it irrelevant, but I tell you that if you fail to take this into consideration, your credit score may suffer. A very good example comes to mind here. If you want to purchase a new car and you buy an "educational" (car sold to consumers, but not used by lenders) or another type of credit score which is premature for your own information. The score you would receive would be definitely different from the score the borrower is looking at. Every borrower, bank or credit company has separate lending standards. A particular credit score may earn you a good deal from one lender but not from another.

Having the thought that all credit scores forecast the same thing: Knowing this, may add to the confusion from the last point but know that we would rectify this in the next chapter, for now,there are models which predict other things than general credit risk. For the scoring models, they can be forecasted or predicted on almost anything which includes all or some of the following:

- Insurance Risk: Yes, insurance risk greatly affects and predicts your credit score. It is no new news that most insurance companies utilize credit scoring models to predict whether or not you are liable to file an auto or homeowner's insurance claim. Any poor insurance score could mean that you will pay higher premiums.
- Revenue Potential: Credit card companies aim to generate revenue not

to lend out money for lending sake. Your revenue scoring models could be used by credit card companies to calculate or foretell whether or not you will use their credit card and most importantly create more revenue for them.

- Response Rates: Sometimes, you would check your mail and then you would see "pre-approved" offers of credit. This is no coincidence, and it is not just something sent randomly. The real deal is that you have been selected from several millions of other individuals to receive that offer due to the fact that you have a "Response Score" which shows that you are more likely to reply to such an offer than anyone else.

- Collectability: Some individuals have collections as part of their credit report. This means that collection agencies are assigned to accumulate the past due debts and thereby to score you to decide whether or not you are likely to reimburse your collection debt sooner than others.

- Fraud Potential: These scoring models have become so sophisticated that they can actually predict whether or not you are trying to make a fraudulent purchase with your credit card. The most surprising thing or amazing thing about this is that it takes just a few minutes to check-out at a store, but within these short amount of time, the serious calculation is going on because you may have been scored to see whether the retailer should accept your credit card or not.

- Bankruptcy potential: The bankruptcy scores hypothesize the chances that you will file for personal bankruptcy. Having a poor bankruptcy score can cause your credit applications to be declined. You may think being bankrupt happens to companies and individuals who own businesses. Well, the ugly head of bankruptcy could show itself on the financial aspect of every individual. And when you have the potential to "become broke" at any given time, no credit card company, loaner or bank would want to give you funds.

When you don't understand your right under the fair credit reporting act: The "FCRA," as it is usually called is a list of credit reporting regulations and rules which direct lenders as well as credit reporting agencies. As a credit conscious individual, you should become familiar with your rights and also the "permissible purposes" as well under which your credit reports can be viewed. You have rights to dispute errors on your credit reports- we would talk about that later, and you also have right to a free copy of your credit reports from each of the three credit reporting agencies. These are your rights, and it is very important that you should know them.

When you fail to realize that you have 3 credit reports and equivalent Credit Scores: Most individuals have the understanding that a credit report exists. But they don't know that an individual has three credit reports which are successfully compiled and maintained by three independent competing companies known as the "credit reporting agencies." These companies store your credit history and even sell them to lenders and consumers likewise. The three largest are; Experian, TransUnion, and Equifax. Each credit report is used to calculate many different credit scores so you should not be on the assuming side that your credit report and scores are all similar.

How To Never Worry About Life's Chaos Again

Well, you wouldn't need to worry about life's chaos if you have enough in the bank. But the most surprising thing is that even when individuals stumble upon a huge sum of money or even win a lottery after some few months, they are back to how they were before. Well, the process is quite simple. First, they start by enjoying my life strategy. Not really a strategy but a principle. An inherent principle entrenched to the minds of those who have that poverty mentality. A modern person should invest 50% of his/her income but what happens is that we find it hard to save and harder to invest because you would use what you have to get more. It is safe and true to say that savings would fetch you more money, but we both know that we only save to have that extra money to spend when unplanned needs arise.

Sometimes when we have so many funds that wouldn't need us to worry about life's chaos again, we squander all of it and our rat race resumes. In this chapter, you would be exposed to the power of savings. Yes, I am aware that you know what savings are all about, you have probably read Rich Dad, Poor Dad by Robert Kiyosaki or any other popular book. I am sure you are aware of the fact that savings can push you from poverty to wealth. However, what happens is that we have that goal, but it never comes into fruition. Let me explain the simple process of how we dump all knowledge into that recessive mind of ours. You read a book about savings. You are inspired. Oh, I want to start saving, yes, I really need to do something. The book goes further to provide you with enough strategies to help you. You finish the book, and you are excited. Let's start saving! The first month, you struggle to save some money. The second month becomes harder than the first. Next, something comes up, and you use all your savings for it. Oh, no! This is not what I planned for. Then you start all over again. I must do this. I really need to do this. You save for three months consecutively and again you make use of the funds for something else. Then you give up. You literarily don't care anymore. This is impossible; let's live life the way it should be, not worrying about tomorrow. Yes, it is true that you shouldn't worry about tomorrow, but those who prepare and plan for the future always find themselves in the best situations. Yes, plans may fail but when you shoot for the stars, you can end up reaching the moon, and that is not bad also. When the rainy day comes what should you do? Keep some, spend some, spend some and spend what you've kept in the future because you're broke. The truth is that most people have that saving mentality. We want to save, but we find it hard to do so.

Every month, you dream of spending just a little bit of money in your budget and taking that second honeymoon or vacation. After making all those plans and fantasizing about them, you wouldn't have enough money to make them a reality. When people think of financial planning, they place savings for retirement or emergencies at the forefront only to relegate it later on. While these are essential to ensuring that you never face that financial ruin, having a rainy day fund can and must be very important for unexpected situations which are short term in nature and those little dreams would become possible.

Starting to save for a rainy day is not rocket science. You should just understand some familiar principles and put them into practice. First, you should understand that a little goes a long way. If your car breaks down today, would you have extra cash on hand to fix it? The fact remains that when most individuals start saving for that rainy day they become discouraged and the funds wouldn't be for the rainy day any longer but for any use. Most times we think that we need to contribute that large sum of money to savings every day. That is the first mistake we make. We don't need to go big. Just start small. That small portion from each check you get can go a long way. Make every day count and make every week count also. As long as you are consistent you'll be fine.

The next thing to do is to automate your savings. Most employers would be happy to help save for that rainy day if you ask them to do so. If you have that right paperwork filled out, you would be able to arrange it. When your savings is automated, you would be able to reach your goals at all cost. Most times you wouldn't even know the difference after your savings has been deducted because you would be building your budget on your current income and you wouldn't know when you begin to cut cost. Furthermore, it is ideal for you to contribute to windfalls. In the sense that it would be difficult for you to spend that unexpected money which is not related to your income or savings, things like a bonus, tax return or maybe a birthday gift. That urge to spend it should be suppressed. Place it in your savings account immediately.

A rainy day fund serves two major purposes. First, it helps you prepare for that short term financial crises, and it also provides you with that opportunity to live your dreams also. Creating a budget is also a good way to achieve this. Even on your phone, you can create a budget. There are several software which could help you with that. Creating your budget shouldn't be the problem but following it would always prove challenging. The best way to start saving for that rainy day is, to begin with, automated savings, using windfalls and taking advantage of several online saving tools just like budgeting software, etc.

Experts claim that you should have anywhere between three to six months' expenses saved up as an emergency fund. Well, I would agree with that because the more you have been able to save up, the more secure you would feel when an emergency comes your way.

Creating an extra source of income is also a good way to get that rainy day fund. Think of it this way that the more money you have, the more money you can save. When you are in the business world, the best way to save is to input money into several operations. The beauty about this is that you don't save only; your money keeps working for you. Are we getting near investment? Yes. Maybe.

It is not hard or complicated to figure out how you spend your money. You understand math to a certain degree, and you understand how to follow a budget. Now, it is a nice idea if you can do this yourself instead of getting someone. Wait, do people get others to help draft out their personal budget? Well, doing it yourself makes you understand how best the number works. You'll know what is going on instead of you to assume what is going on and you'll be able to create that perfect set up for yourself. Tracking what goes out and what comes in is the ground process of any business in this world. When you understand that there is actually much value to your time, you wouldn't want to spend it reading so many printouts or piles of document (if your business requires you to do so) but instead you would begin to concern yourself with the process of budgeting making the right rows for the months and the columns for the income as well as expenses. This principle works for personal use as well as corporate use. However, in the business world, you would have a very complex budget still based on the fundamental principles of budgeting. The fundamentals would have a column for; Gross revenue: where your money is coming from then expenses; where your money is going followed by the Net income: how much I left for you.

Taking a look at what you have, you should understand that the key is to make every expense accountable and measurable also. You should figure out which expenses are essential and the ones that are not. Learn to cut the fat. Your budget should be placed in a place where you can see it daily. Revisit it regularly and make a weekly meeting to visit your team to review the business process for that week. The twenty minutes you spend reviewing your budget could save you twenty thousand in the future.

Hefty expenses occur all the time. You may need a new car, a bigger house or you may just decide to go back to school to get your degree. How do people who find themselves in this situation react? The first thing they do is to go into debt once again. If you have a budget, this shouldn't be a problem because funds from a rainy day would help you. If you don't have a budget, then you are spending without thinking. Yes, read that again because when you become broke in the middle of the month, you wouldn't be able to track your expenses.

Okay, you may be thinking; I have a budget, but I find it very hard to stick with it. Well, that happens because you don't understand how budgeting can improve your financial life. If you do understand how important it is to keep that budget, you would protect it and stick to it at all cost. However, if you are struggling with sticking to your budget, I would provide you with some few strategies.

First, you should focus on your savings. Aren't we tired of talking about savings? No, because it is very important. Make saving money a priority in your life. When you create your budget using that your personal finance software, you should learn to cut cost to save each month and set aside some funds from your paycheck. The surprising thing about savings is that it doesn't depend on how much you are earning but how much you are willing to save. Some might be earning millions but find it hard to save some while some might be earning hundreds, but they have that saving culture. Okay, they are saving because they are broke. If you go with this perception, you are completely wrong. He who is faithful over little would be faithful when it comes to having that big task. Those having little plus a good saving culture would have easy lives when they start earning big.

Furthermore, you should learn to use cash. Stay away from credit cards. Don't just walk into a store to make a purchase using a credit card. When you are using cash, you would understand how important savings is because just seeing the paper leaving your hands is enough to force you to save, especially when it is your hard-earned currency. You should learn to take a certain amount of cash out of your account each week which you would spend on gas, food and those extra expenses might not be needed all the time.

Another step you can take to stick to your budget is to cut out the bad habits. While you may be enjoying drinking, smoking, partying or just having fun you shouldn't make an expensive lifestyle become a habit. Learn to cut out bad habits. Yes, it is good to live large if you can afford it. If you can't, leave the Gucci Shoes and bags for now. When you are financially stable enough, you'll get them. Don't go broke trying to be rich. You don't need to be who you are not. Sharing your budgeting responsibilities isn't a bad idea also. It would help you stick to it. You may have a roommate or a family. Spending habits should be monitored. You should learn to stop spending money haphazardly. Sit down and wok out that budget together with your family, friend your personal finance software and even your entire household.

Save $1000 in a month.

Let us tell the truth. Americans suck at saving money. Not only Americans though Africans, Asians and citizens of the world in general. Most times, we really don't know how to identify the long term investment goals and satisfy them. Instead, we go into debt and heap the blame on every other person because we don't see what is wrong in borrowing money or spending excessively. The truth is that we want to know how to save money, but we don't want to really save money. We care less about proper asset allocation, and we don't want to bother ourselves about the stock market returns. All we just care about is the money we have right now. The #save $1000 a monthis put together not to provide that stupid frugal tips but to expose you to that life of savings and the benefits of putting money away for a while. Why start with something big? Or why jump into this idea? First, saving $1 per week or $10 per week is cool. However, it is not challenging, and it is not worth changing your behavior. Yes, if you really want to change something. Make it big! So that the difference can be obvious. Saving $1000 in 30 days is okay, it is big, and when the results come, you'll find out that you've not just wasted your time, but you've been able to accomplish something great. You should start this only if you're serious.

If or when you save $1000 a month you would have $12,000 in a year. In 20 years you would have $240,000 if you are just saving alone, nothing else. However, do you know that if you invest your savings in the sixth or even in the third month, you can become a millionaire in the space of three years while you are still keeping those savings of yours?Yes, it is possible. Let's do that quick math. During the sixth month, you would have $6000. If you invest that amount, you can be receiving interest of $1000 every month if you play your cards right. You would gain an extra $12000 from investment in one year. The beauty about investment is that you can start small, get big and still continue until it becomes bigger and bigger. You can make use of the part in the $12,000 to invest, or you put in all of it. With the proper stock, you can get up to $54,000 in a year. Multiply that amount by 10 (ten years) you'll get $540,000 in ten years. It wouldn't be smart of you if you wait till you have $540,000 before investing again you can make use of the $54,000 and gain $648,000 in a year. Multiply that amount by just two years. You'll have $1,296,000. Convinced?

The secret to investing is to forget that your money is someone else working for you. It may be hard and not easy I tell you but after you place that investment you'll never regret it. Saving is a huge step towards financial freedom and investment is one of the best ways to become rich beyond your thinking in a short while. Furthermore, you should learn to hold yourself capable of your incompetence.

Stock Market Terminologies

You are a beginner, that is cool because even the experts were once like you. Having said that, it would be inconsiderate of me if I fail to speak or relate to your own level of knowledge. That is why this chapter was just chipped in so that you can understand all the jargons. We are aware that the stock market is simply an exchange that gives people that opportunity and space to purchase and sell stocks. Well, the stock exchange is just buying and selling in disguise. I would list some terminologies which I think would be very helpful.

1. Annual report. The annual report is what a company presents which contains information about the company and its cash flow. The funny thing here is that annual report isn't meant for stock market alone.

2. Averaging Down. As an investor, you may decide to buy more of a stock as the

price goes down. This means that the amount you use in purchasing, your average purchasing decreases. People do this when they expect that the stock would rebound later.

3. Beta: This is the relationship between the price of a stock and the movement of the market. A market moves. It is either things are getting cheaper or costlier. So let us say if stock XYZ has a beta of 1.5 what this means is that stock XYZ has a beta of 1.5

4. Broker: A broker is an individual who sells an investment for you and receives a commission.

5. Dividend is a part of the company's earnings that are paid to shareholders, or those individuals who own that company's stock. It is paid on a quarterly or annual basis.

6. Index. The index is what is used as that citation or reference marker for investors. Portfolio managers would

also take a good look at the index before thinking of managing your stock. Popular examples are the Standard & Poor's 500 and Dow Jones Industrial Average.

7. Portfolio: The portfolio is a collection of investments which is owned by an investor and makes up his/her portfolio. However, you can have an infinite amount of stocks and even other securities.

8. Volatility: this has to do with the price of a stock or the stock market as an entity. Stocks that are highly volatile are those who are extreme and have daily up and down movements. Stocks that are considered volatile are Stocks that are delicate and carefully traded. They also have low trading volumes.

9. Moving average: A stock's average price per share which is used during that specific period of time is known as the moving average. You should be able to

study some common time frames of study which has to do with terms of a stock's moving average which includes 50 and 200-day moving averages.

10. Close. The NYSE and Nasdaq closed at 4 p.m., but the after-hours trading would continue until 8 p.m. the close just means that there is a time which a stock exchange closes to trading.

Introduction To The Stock Market

What is the stock market? Wikipedia defines the stock market as a market or equity market which is a public entity. Now you may be thinking, what is stock or what are stocks? Not to introduce some business jargons again, just know that stocks are that entity that shows that you own a company or part of a company. The stock market is the biggest market in the world. As an investor or potential investor, you'll need to understand some popular topics which would help you in your investing career.

First, you must become an avid reader of quality investing news, business news, information and all other news vital to your success as a new stock exchange investor. Yes, you can learn about the stock exchange market you can begin trading stocks and risking your own very cash if you don't have the knowledge. There is a lot to learn, and you can never know it all. The next thing to do is to identify your investing objective. Make sure you have an objective. That investment goal is very important. It shouldn't be vague like: I want to be the richest investor, or I want to make much money from investing. That is vague and unacceptable. You should be specific, and your goals should be SMART. In the space of three years, I want to make $120,000 through passive investment. Are your goals realistic? What happens is that many people who go into stock market investment especially as beginners feel that stock market exchange is a good way to make quick money, so they focus more on the short-term investment. This shouldn't be the case a long term strategy is the better choice when it comes to stock exchange.

Furthermore, you need to determine what kind of investment trader you would choose to be. This book is centered on passive investment. So you'll most likely be a passive investor than someone who scalp shares, buys and hold stocks for a long term or swing trades. You should understand that there are levels to this. The knowledge and the understanding must be solid else you'll lose money.

It wouldn't be too early for us to introduce passive income investing. You can continue to do the same thing and expect a different result. Building that passive income would always remain the best way to free yourself from the shackles of financial bondage. But we should note that sometimes we don't create passive income, we just follow it's flow while some would take much initial effort to start because you would need to purchase some assets. Amidst all these, one thing is sure, when it starts giving you income, it never stops.

Basically, there are two types of income sources: Active or earned income and Passive income which is also known as residual income. We know that active income is basically the money you earn as an employee or self-employed individual. This income is linear in nature, meaning that if you stop working, the income stops also. A major disadvantage about active income is that one has to put in a lot of time and energy to maintain it and as frustrating as it could sound, the time and energy you put into it may not worth it.

Throughout the previous chapter, we have been able to prove that financial success hinges on two things: having enough income to support your desired lifestyle, two, having enough time to do what you want. When you own an active income stream, you exchange time for money. Active income alone is not an effective way to create wealth. What you need is passive income.

This type of income is very important for financial freedom because it is money earned irrespective of whether you actively work or not. You are literarily making money in your sleep. You work as a wealth creator building a business using income-generating assets.

What's an asset? Anything that makes money for you. Yes, we can make money while we sleep; however, passive income is not completely hands off.

There are several passive income opportunities like:

1. Real estate (rental income)
2. Franchising
3. Royalties (from books or music)
4. Licensing fees (from products created by you)
5. Affiliate marketing
6. Online advertising revenue
7. Business revenue from selling your own products and services.

Thank God for property and internet business models. Everything listed above can be executed rightly without much learning. Our generation today has made multiple income streams doable for everybody. This process is a tested and trusted one.

Come to think of it. We really don't have any suggestion on how to create that passive income. But you can take the following steps;

- ✓ You can start a blog
- ✓ Create an online course
- ✓ Build an app
- ✓ Write an eBook
- ✓ Create a website and sell products
- ✓ Rent out your tools

The suggestion could go on and on. It all depends on the method you want to employ. I would list a few methods here.

First, don't be a landlord; be an investor. A landlord would sit on the income he is receiving from renting just one apartment. An investor would think of more than just one apartment. He/she would invest in more than one business enterprise.

Don't build an active income for your passive funds. Confused? Let me explain this. You are receiving $1500 a month from your housing investment. What is expected of you is to put that money to work, not keep it in the bank to accrue minute interest?

Furthermore, you are going to be learning practical methods from me on how to tap into the provision of passive income to become financially free.

1. Save Like Nobody Owes You Anything. Right from the beginning of this book, we have stated the importance of savings. It should be noted that when your money starts working for you, you shouldn't spend it all. Invest in other business and save a lot. If you fail to build your overall "Money strength" through the use of some special financial nut, you may fall back to where you started. However, it is important that the savings I am referring to are After-tax savings. What you need to do is save money after contributing your 401K (retirement savings plan

sponsored by an employer) and IRAs since you can't safelytouch funds in the pre-tax retirement's accounts until you're 59.5. What I did was that I saved 50-70% of my tax, after 401K contribution every year for 13 years because I was speculating that I wouldn't last for 20 years with my finance. Now, I save 100% of my passive income

2. Find something you love doing and make it a source of income. I love writing and investing. That is why you have this book in your hands. I combined these two interest with my ability to get things done. What did I get? Multiple investment opportunities. Every individual has that field of strength. A place that is very comfortable for them, it could be playing a sport, doing a kind of work, etc. You just need to open your mind to the opportunities around

3. Treat Passive Income Like A Game. Remember the previous chapter; an active income could serve as the beginning step for the passive income. The initial funding has to come from somewhere. So this is what I mean when I say you should treat it as a game. Don't rush; take it as a journey with different levels. Just like playing a game. If you fail in level one, it is not the end of the game as you have an active income and you can restart.

4. Determine What Income Level Will Make You Happy. This leads us back to our initial goal. You break down your goals into smaller bits. You must have made this decision even before you go into the venture which would provide the passive income.

5. Don't force yourself to start. When you force yourself, things won't work out naturally.

For some, financial freedom has a good job that pays well every month. And having much excess which they can use to buy fancy cars, a bigger house, or nice vacations. Being able to pay off debt, having a healthy emergency fund and money in the bank account to fund their kid's college. While others believe that financial freedom is number one. They look to sock away a nest egg of $3 million, $4 million, or whatever their number might be. It all begins with you. Make use of the principles in this book. And the sky would just be a starting point.

Passive Index Investment

Passive income is the easiest type of investment. Anyone can literally retire a millionaire with this right strategy making use of passive index investment. However, you should learn to take some hours to pick the winners in this field and follow their footsteps. The simplest and easiest way to make money is by tracking the market. Tracking has to do with monitoring the market. First, we really need to understand what index funds are and how we can start investing as a beginner.

Index funds are now becoming a major force in the investing world. Research has been able to show us that in 2016, more than $1 out of every $5 invested in the stock exchange market was conducted using the index fund. As a new investor is this your concern? Yes. It is because you would need to understand what index funds are, the weaknesses and it's advantages because you must be ready to face all these questions and give a good response because this is the foundation of this book and given that you are a smaller investor you should give index funds a proper look. Briefly, I would talk about index funds; the good, the bad and the horrible. Knowing this would extend your horoscope.

First, what are index funds? To understand what index funds is you should view it from an academic aspect. Basically, it has to do with a person or a committee of people sitting down and coming up with that list of rules of how to build or create a portfolio of individual holdings because when it all comes to that end, the only thing left that you can actually invest in is the single common stocks or bonds. Are you confused? Are you confused? I hope not. Let me give you the example of the most famous index of all time; the Dow Jones Industrial Average which is a list of thirty blue-chip stocks. This list is created by the representative collection of stocks which are pivotal to the economy of the U.S. These shares are weighted next based on stock price and adjustments also. Therefore making way for things such as stock splits.Stocks like these are selected by the editors of the standard Wall Street Journal

& P 500 and even other indices have been overtaken by the Dow Jones Industrial Average. Even over longer periods of time by a meaningful margin based on compounded functions even though the year-to-year results deviates and seems to appear small. We made mention of the S&P f500 which is now the most widely discussed index in the world. The S&P 500 stands for Standard and Poor's 500. It was called the composite index in 1932, but it then expanded to 90 stocks three years later before counting up to 500 in 1957. The S&P 500 has that complex methodology than the Dow Jones Industrial Average. However, inthe past decade, the S&P 500's methodology has changed drastically. The inexperienced investors may find it hard to understand because it is not like the way it used to be in the past. Don't be tired; all these jargons and terminologies would lead to something meaningful.

Investors today are mostly clueless. They really don't know what they are going into. That is why it is very important that you know what you are going into or else you would enter a ship of Theseus paradox and you would wonder what point you are going to face because you can't wrap your head around what is happening.

You should just have it at the back of your mind that an index fund is simply a mutual fund. Instead of you to have that portfolio manager making a choice for you, outsourcing that capital allocation job to that individual or committee would determine the index methodology. The Jones Industrial Average index fund or ETF (exchange traded fund) is a mutual fund which trades like that share of stock throughout the day rather than settling at the end of the day like that ordinary fund. Most times it is the same portfolio and even the same underlying holdings. What you are just doing in simple terms is that you're handing over the job of managing your money to professional editors of The Wall Street Journal. When you buy an S&P 500 index fund, you're just giving the job of handling your money to a handful of people at Standard and Poors. At the long run, it would end in your own portfolio as your individual stock, or it would just be held in a pooled structure with a portfolio manager over it who is responsible for getting the result as close to the index as possible this is known as tracking.

Psychology Of Investment

We are aware that the study of economics and finance is traditionally the assumption that people always behave rationally. However, it is not the case in reality. People behave irrationally. Yes, take that from me. They act or do things which are not of their best interest. The behavioral finance is that combination of psychology and the financial theory also. This is now becoming an academic discipline, and there are several articles which talk about this online. However, they all fail to understand that people make mistakes and those mistakes aren't mistakes they are just wrong decisions for that particular time.

Furthermore, emotional factors such as fear, uncertainty, personal bias, regret aversion, and ego can play so much importance in the life of an investor. Despite efforts to be sensible in monetary matters, we still fall into the same problem and mistakes because of these psychological factors. Experts say that there are cognitive principles which affect our decision making when it comes to money matters. Psychological issues like regret aversion, ego, and personal bias affect the stock market and investment like any other factor. In this chapter, I have been able to draw raw data from these attitudes.

Having said that, one of the most important psychological issues I feel should be treated first is the issue of consistency. When the market falls, do you fold? What happens when issues are not going as planned. What do you do? You have to understand the mindset of an investor to be able to know how investment really works. You can have the mind of an investor, and you wouldn't have any investment. There are several people who just place money into what they feel would work and it would happen that they would get enough money in several folds. But the regret aversion is also a strong psychological issue.

We hate losing and it takes an asymmetrical attitude to risk it all. When you are faced with losses what do you do? Do you prepare to admit that we have made a mistake or do we begin to assume that losing make us better investors?In the same manner, when we experience gains what do we do? We have that strong attitude, and we boast of how things worked our way right? Common sense should tell us that winners sell to the losers. Sometimes it is senseless to hang on to a stock when it is not doing well right? Well, it is good to be senseless at times. If you so much believe in that stock, you should not be tempted to double up on it.

More also, the rule of thumb and overconfidence are also two psychological products which affect an investor. Some investors, including professionals, tend to be overly confident in their ability to make the right decision. Well, it extends from many things we do in our everyday life. Investors seem to be clearly overconfident of their abilities and accuracy of their predictions. Making an investment is not a bet. It is okay to be prudent and objective in manner. You should learn how to make mistakes and improve. The rule of thumb is also a psychological factor which affects the investor. The rule of thumb requires an investor to hold a stock that has done well before but id doing badly now, thinking that it would go back to how it was before.

Lastly, the house money effect. Okay, things are going well; your investment is yielding so much. Then you feel like, why can't I add more, I should make it bigger than before. If an investor has that good run with some investments, he/she is tempted to take one higher level of risk with future investment. Well, the truth remains that not all similar principles have similar solutions. There are a few strange cases.

How To Purchase Index Funds

Warren Buffet, the greatest investor in the history of the stock market and even one of the richest people in the history of America, is attributed to a saying that investors should know their limitations. Well, those words are very simple and easy to understand and apply in everyday life. However, you should know what you are capable of doing and what you can't do. Ask yourself if you got a chance to fight with that grizzly bear. You say that this is crazy because the bear is big and it would probably kill you but do you get that picture? Are you doing more than you can? Are you biting off more than you can chew? There are a lot of people on Wall Street that are successful. Those who fight bears and bulls every day and they overcome. Oh, yes, I know. This chapter is not about bears and bulls. But if you are thinking of purchasing an index fund, you

79

should be ready to become the bear or the bull. As a new investor, nothing beats index funds because they are simple and secure ways to invest and prosper in the stock market. Index funds allow investors to relax. Is it a secure way to allow some individuals to take your burdens right? Whether investing on your own or taking advantage of index funds, you should know your limitations.

The index mutual funds are laisezz-fair, easy, low-cost and cover a large horoscope of stock investment. There are three simple steps to follow if you want to purchase index funds.

- Decide where to buy
- Pick an index
- Check investment minimum and another cost.

Chose where to buy the index fund. You chose to purchase that index fund directly from a mutual fund company or a brokerage any decision you make is fine. Same goes for the exchange-traded funds now. Let us hit the nail on the head. Fund selection. Is the first thing that should be Where do you want to buy them? From various fund families? From the big mutual fund companies? You must carry out that selection, and you must not limit everything to what is available or a discount broker's lineup. Furthermore, you should also consider convenience. Looking for a single provider who is ready to accommodate all your needs, for example, is very important to make sure that your mutual funds become okay. If you're just going to invest in a mutual fund or you are going for a mix of funds you should find a mutual fund company able to serve you that investment hub. But if you need such sophistication in your stock research, you need to go out and do that yourself. Pick that research and screening tool, that discount broker who sells index funds. You may even need to open a brokerage account. When picking where to buy you should remember that there is also commission-free options.

There are kinds of options do not offer transaction-fee mutual funds or commission-free ETFs. Don't forget that selecting or picking discount brokers would definitely affect the success of your investment. The selection should be from Charles Schwab, E-Trade, Fidelity and TD Ameritrade. They are all worth checking out. Lastly, the trading cost should also be another factor that you should consider when deciding to buy funds. If the commission or transaction of the fee isn't waived, think of how much a broker or fund company would charge you to buy or sell the index fund. These mutual fund commissions are higher than the stock trading ones. Some would be $20.

Picking an index. The index of mutual funds would track various indexes. The Standard & Poor's 500 index is one of the best-known indexes because it has that permanent 500 companies it tracks which includes several large, and well known U.S- based businesses. I don't think I have been able to see an index having more than that. But we should know that the S&P 500 is not the only index in town. There are several other indexes which are based on the composition of stock and other assets also like the company size and capitalization, geography, business sector or industry, asset types, and even the market opportunities.

Even though there are arrays of choices, you should need to know the one that would be perfect for you. Warren Buffet did say that the average investor needs only invest in a broad stock market index to be properly diversified.

Checking investment minimum and the other cost is also very important. The low cost is one of the biggest selling points of index funds. Because the truth is that nobody wants to spend much to make much. Well, that is the truth. The investments are easy and cheap to run because they have that automated structure. It follows with the shifts in value in an index. However, you shouldn't assume that all value in an index are cheap or cost low. Sometimes, they may not be actively managed by a team of a well-paid analyst but still, carry administrative costs. This cost would be subtracted from each fund shareholder's returns as that percentage of the overall investment. You should consider the following during the checking investment process:

- Investment minimum: The smallest fund required to invest could go as low as a few thousand ($2000). However, once you've been able to cross that threshold, most investors would definitely want to add more money in smaller increments.

- Account minimum: The brokerage's account minimum is $0, and it is common for customers who open a traditional or Roth (IRA). But you should understand that there is a big difference between investment minimum and account minimum.

- Expense ratio. It is one of the main cost which is subtracted from each fund a shareholder returns as the percent of the overall investment. You can find the expense ratio in that mutual fund prospectus or when you call up a quote of a mutual fund on any financial site. The annual expense ratio was 09% for the stock index funds and 0.07% for the bond index funds. Furthermore, you should understand the tax-cost ratio which is in addition to paying fees, owning the fund could also trigger capital gain taxes if it is held outside tax-advantaged accounts like a 401(k) or the IRA.

Portfolio Ideas

In this chapter, you would be exposed to different kinds of portfolio ideas. It is not really an idea but a standardized process. However, we can't possibly go into the portfolio ideas without talking about the portfolio types. There are different types of portfolio types, I wouldn't go into all, but I would only talk about those that concern us as index investors.

The first portfolio that should be on this list is the aggressive portfolio. As the name sounds; It is aggressive. You'll be facing stocks that are high in risk and also high reward also — coupled with that fact that the stocks in this category would either help you have that high beta, or it would reduce it. Stocks which have high beta continually experience fluctuations. This means that they are not stable and their instability has so much to do with the overall market.Individuals having aggressive stock offerings in the early stages of growth always have that unique value proposition. If you intend to build that portfolio you should look for common household names, check online for companies which are rapidly accelerating earnings. This would require you to scrutinize that technology but many firms in other sectors would be pursuing that same thing as well.

Furthermore, the defensive portfolio is also another type of portfolio. This is when you put defensive stocks in your harem. What this suggests is that you don't have a high beta stock in your portfolio. These kind of stocks are not prone to instability. The income portfolio is also another kind of portfolio. But this one deals with making money from the dividends and other types of stakeholders and distributors. This looks like the defensive stocks, but instead of having a lower income, it would offer you higher yields. Furthermore, the income portfolio brings positive cash flow as well as the Real Estate Invest Trust (REITs).

87

MLP (Master Limited Partnership) and many more are excellent avenues for getting those income-producing investment.

If you are looking for an investment that is the closest thing to pure gamble, you have a speculative portfolio. Just as it sounds, it is speculative, rough, tentative. And since it is just like a gamble, you have more risk involved than any other portfolio discussed here. The investor gurus have suggested that out of one's investable assets, 10% falls under the speculative. You might want to be of the opinion that the widespread of Leverage ETFs in the recent market happens because of the high increase in the speculative portfolios. This may be true, but we should not forget that this kind of portfolio requires so much attention and carefulness, therefore, picking the right investment would require a special kind of skill something I believe most people don't have. Speculative stocks require so much study and attention to every detail.

You might be thinking of shaping your portfolio to the hybrid level. The hybrid is the combination of several investments like bonds, commodities, real estate, art, just anything you can think of that can fetch you money in the long run. Following the regular principle of investment, this type of portfolio would entail blue-chip stocks and even have some high-grade government corporate bonds entrenched in it. REITs and MLP's would not be left out too. Fundamentally, what a hybrid portfolio would have is that beautiful and low-risk mix of different stocks and bonds in different sizes and proportions, but all remained fixed. Since you're dipping your hands into several investments and blending them perfectly, you are actively involved in diversification. Furthermore, an approach like this would give so many benefits due to the equities and the fixed income securities.

For the indexfunds portfolios, there are three simple portfolio strategies. First is the *two fund portfolio* which includes two major funds; the global stock market fund and the U.S investment grade bond. Both are vanguard funds which blend into the total Bond Market ETF (Ticker: BND), and this holds the mortgage securities also.

We shouldn't forget our lazy people. That is why we have a lazy portfolio. It is good to be lazy. Laziness brings out that creativity and it would make you complete a job of two weeks in two days because of too much procrastination on your part. This portfolio is divided into two; the U.S only fund and the international fund also. Making use of this strategy, an individual would be able to regulate the amount of U.S dollar investments. The dollar is a global currency. I am sure you know that right?

The last is The core 4 Portfolio. This kind or type of portfolio is carved out of the U.S commercial real estate and has a separate class. The commercial real estate's makes up about 13 percent of the U.S. economy and yet represents only 3 percent of the stock market, maybe because the stock market has the highest number of gurus. And another reason why I think this happens is that most commercial real estate is privately owned rather than that scrutinized tradable investment from the government.

Basics Of FIRE

Fire? Let's get the extinguisher. FIRE (Financial Independence and early retirement). That sound better right? Well, for now, Fire is having that moment. It is not hard to understand, and it is not hard to appeal. Financial independence sounds cool. There is nothing as good as being your own boss. You'll be able to go on vacation and do what you like. The Fire movement is something that quickly gains momentum. Now, you're thinking, what is Fire exactly?

Well, when you are thinking of your retirement age, you probably think that it would be in the '50s or '60s. Well, that is good. However it is the norm, and the social security administration would only allow you to start taking benefits at age 62. Take for example you can start to get your funds from your retirement account without penalty at age 59 ½ .

Even though we are aware of that retirement age, it is advisable for us to start FIRE very early especially when we are in our 30's or 40's. Some even start in their 20's. Early retirement is the major aim of FIRE, but there is more to it than that.

Financial independence ultimately means that you can shape your life without taking money into consideration, most of us have to consider our finances in nearly every decision we make, or maybe even make decision solely based on money. But once we reach financial independence, we get the freedom not to be bossed around by what we earn or what we have saved. A good reason to retire early is that you have an alternate vision for your life that you are eager to pursue, but which you can't pursue while employed full time, Achieving financial independence allowed us to leave that career chapter of our lives from a place of gratitude and appreciation, and move onto our next chapter that we're in control of

- Tanja Hester, a recent FIRE graduate and founder of the website Our Next Life.

I am sure you're still wondering what really is this Fire? It is a movement which follows one simple rule; spend less than you earn and save difference in low-fee investments like index funds- Hester.

The beauty about Fire is that it is a retirement plan which wants you to retire early.

"Retiring early because you don't like your job is a bad reason to do it and is a recipe for being bored or aimless when you get there," she said. "Achieving FIRE is a big deal, and it takes a lot of focus and determination. It's not for those who want to get rich quick, or for those who just hate their job. The better solution then is just to find a new job or a new career path. I'm a huge believer that you can love your job and still want to retire early or just achieve financial independence! That was true for us. We loved our work, the people we worked with, and our clients, but we didn't love the pace of it, the pressure or the constant travel."- Hayes, another graduate of FIRE

We shouldn't forget that other sources of income are important parts of these financial freedom process. Because the less money you need to live, the less money you need to save in order to fund the rest of your years. Let us do the math:

To highlight the value of cutting expenses, for every $100 per month you can trim, it means you need $30,000 less to achieve FI ($1,200 yearly expense x 25 = $30,000).

The three basic elements to FIRE are; time, expenses and income. However, the goal is to put that space between the expenses and the income making sure that you spend little while you gain more. The rules are quite easy, and you'll definitely want to jump on it but getting there, attaining that level can be a problem if you are not ready to leave that disciplined life.

The only way to have that strong determination is to have a strong why. Hayes did say. "If you want to retire early, you need to have a strong 'why Do you want to quit your job so that you can start that business you always talked about with your friends? Do you want to have more than two weeks per year of vacation time? Do you want to spend more time with your loved ones? Whatever you're why to let that be the motivating factor to create a plan and stick to it during the tough times. Once you have that why you want to determine your path."

You should be very specific about what you want and how you're going to get there. The truth is that this book, all of it centers on the most fundamental principles which you know, and you've been listening to since childhood. SAVINGS.

Do not save what is left after spending, but spend what is left after saving – Warren Buffet

Power Of Compound Interest

"The most powerful force in the universe is compound interest."

-Albert Einstein

That quote shouldn't be from a science prodigy, guru and legend. What does he know about compound interest? Well, investment, a stock market, and stock exchange are simple math and probability. That is not my concern though.

Ask any individual about compound interest and you'll hear him/her say; yeah, I know it. I know little or something about it. Well, if you truly understand compound interest, you wouldn't be where you are now. You wouldn't have so much bad credit and a lot of debts from credit cards. The sad truth is that the financial sector makes use of the general public. They want to make millions from you while you suffer to make ends meet.

Compound interest to me should first be explained mathematically. It is interest that is paid on interest and principal over a long period of time. Let's say you have some $10,000 today and you make 3% each year from your bank. You would have $10,300 by the end of the year. If you leave it there for the second year, you would have $10,609 the third year would be $10,927. This is so small, isn't it? But when compound interest comes in you'll have compounded a 10% per year deal and you'll have doubled the money in 7 years. In 28 years you would have about $160,000. $160,000 from $10,000 within two decades and eight years doing nothing. Do you get that?

However, we shouldn't cover our eyes to the fact that credit card charges would work against us and our bank is only teaching us to calculate the interest daily which is supposed to be to our advantage. You see that they make use of your money to get more money while they hand over peanuts to you. Well, mutual funds and stocks, typically only provide yearly dividends. Likewise, the banks on their fixed deposit are yearly also. Very pathetic interest rates. Compounding is a very good way to get the best from your residual funds. Especially funds that you don't intend to spend anytime soon. For compound interest to work, you would need to set that compounding frequency. The more frequent it happens, the better it is. You can start to compound your funds quarterly. Compounding by seconds is ideal, and it is one of the best ways to enjoy compounding, it is better than yearly compounding. Using this incredible force would help you to break the chains of financial restraints. Furthermore, if you want to choose an investment vehicle for compounding, you should make sure that;

- It has excellent returns (minimum of 5%)
- It has frequent compounding (at least monthly)

- Low risk with a high winning percentage is involved. At least 90%
- It allows you to withdraw whatever you want, whenever you want. You can decide to stop anytime you wish.

I keep telling people about taking that particular step as soon as they find it convincing. I would also tell you the same here. Before Bitcoin became what it is today. I remember that there was a time that 1BTC was $105. I wanted to buy it,but I was so skeptical. I feared that it would crash and something might just happen. I pushed it aside and faced other investment opportunities. Fast forward to November 2017, BTC is $10,000. Okay, I knew I had missed the opportunity, but I was so sure that it was going to go down once more. And it was down again. Whatever step you want to take, take it now. You shouldn't sleep on it. Nobody find's a treasure or money buried beneath, wouldn't you dig to find it?

Ever since the 1970's the United States dollars has been following that consistent trend of 5-7 years of cycles of up and down trends. This is not the late 2001 or 2002 leave the money over there then forget about it for a while. That is savings in the simple comment all; it shows that you're the only one thinks about transportation when we are talking about the life and death of a patient.

Starting people is always happy because he walks in and makes a sum grow faster than it was before because she did earpiece, there was an attritionist (Someone would add or place something there.) so the question on your lips. Fist, do you really make $250? Well, definitely been helping her for a while now. Do you know that age 25 group, you'll accumulate $878,570 by age 65? The shorter the wire, the more efficient it is. You should get your body ready for the simplest investment process. As an employee, being faithful to the initial instructions from the doctor but you later fail to understand or follow the rest because you feel that you don't need to.

Selecting Your Asset Allocation

Is Life about balance and choice right? Our investing lives are divided into two broad stages making use of just two funds: the wealth Acquisition stage and the Wealth Preservation stage. But you can simply blend both right?

VTSAX (Vanguard Total Stock Market Index Fund) and VBTLX (Vanguard Total Bond Market Index Fund) are two broad aspects of the indexing funds.

When you are investing with the mentality of wealth acquisition, you are working to gain more money, save and invest again. VTSAX is the most preferred here. Financial independence must be your goal so your savings rate must be high and right also. As you invest that money each month, you allow the market's wild ride go smooth. Then you get into the world of wealth preservations. This is when you decide to step away from your job and the regular paychecks you receive, and you begin to live on only your income from investment. Sounds risky? Yes, because you wouldn't have any extra fund to fall but to incase something happens, however, adding bonds to the portfolio like the fresh cash you'll be investing would help your bonds have that smooth investment ride. In the real world, you might not be able to make the distinction between making some money in retirement and out of retirement because investment shouldn't be about retirement. Remember FIRE right?

However, to create this solid framework of asset allocation, we should know that these two additional factors would provide you with that balance you need.

First, you'll need effort. There was a study which shows that allocation provides the best return over time but it is not the same at all and this suggests that adding a smaller percentage of bonds like 10-20% would outperform the 100% stocks. But you should note that the 100% is an 80/20% mix. How these results would unfold over the years is something that is unpredictable, and for this reason, we should learn to favor simplicity. Having said that if you're willing to put more effort or work hard you can see slightly smooth out the wild ride and you can possibly outperform them over time by adding the 10-25% bonds. If you take this step for once in a year, you would be able to rebalance your funds and to maintain your chosen allocation also. You might also want to rebalance your funds anytime the market makes that major move (20% +) up or down. This would require you to either sell shares in whichever asset class that has performed better or to buy shares in the one lagging.

We all know that basically, what bonds do is to smooth the ride and stocks power the returns. However, the more you hold in stocks, the better your results and the more gut-wrenching volatility you'll need to endure and finally scale through. If you're thinking of holding a stock, you must not think, but you must be mentally tough enough to do this so that you'll not panic when they plunge. And you should not make the mistake that you would own them forever, they would surely plunge, and they would plunge at the most unexpected times.

The Market Must Crash!

Yes, you read that right. The market must crash; in fact, it should crash. In fact, market crashes are to be expected. You are new to what happened in 2008. It had happened before, and it would happen again and again. I have been in the investing game for almost 40 years now, and in that time we've had

- ✓ The great recession of 1974-1975. Some of you wouldn't know this because you're new investors.
- ✓ The massive inflation of the late 1970s & early 1980 also. WIN (Whip Inflation Now). This was when mortgages rates were pushing 20%, and you could buy 10-year treasuries paying just 15%+
- ✓ The infamous 1989 Business week cover which read: *The Death Of Equities*. The death gave rise to the greatest comeback bull market of all time. This didn't stop the crash of

- ✓ 1987. This is one of the Biggest one day drop in history. Many brokers were literally on the window ledges, and even some took that leap.
- ✓ What followed next is the recession of the early '90s.
- ✓ Then the Tech rash of the late '90s
- ✓ Followed by the deadly 9/11
- ✓ Then there was a little dust-up in 2008.

Somehow, the market would always recover. And if someday it really doesn't then there is no investment that would be safe, and none of this financial knowledge and strategies would matter anyway. Looking at the bright side of things, the S&P 500 that broader and more telling index grew at an annualized rate of 11.9%. This means amidst all these, if you had invested $1,000 then you would probably have $89,790 as 2015 dawns that is one of the many impressive results from these disasters. What you need to do is toughen up and let it ride. You should allow that to sink. The stock market and investment are not for the weak. The market would always go up; you should understand that it wouldn't always be a smooth ride. How you take control of that ridiculous increase would determine how you would handle the depressing days also. Take a moment to look at the chart of the stock market over time look at the trend and relentless disaster after and even the disaster up. Notice something? The truth is that the next 10, 20, 30 or 40 years would have so much collapse, recession, and even disasters also. When this is about to happen or when it is happening, you should toughen up and learn to ignore the noise while you stay the course and ride out of the storm.

Funny enough, you should know that bad things are coming, and you should expect them.

Best Index Funds For The Long Term

The best index funds always have low expenses and diversified portfolios which can definitely stand the test of time. But it should be noted that not all index funds are diversified and some are not proper for long-term investment. There is a wide variety of index funds to choose from, and because of this, it is important that an investor should understand the best needs an index fund attracts.

The S&P 500 Index fund is the most popular kind of index fund, but there are different kinds also. First, we have the Vanguard 500 Index (VFINX). This is a mutual fund that is available for the public, and it became active through the mind-blowing business idea of Vanguard investments, Jack Bogle who did study market and also took note that most traders don't beat the average market levels and they have been able to factor the expenses.

Therefore, if by simply buying that low-cost mutual fund which is the basket of stocks found in the index then the investors would be able to capture reasonable returns also. The VFINX has that expense ratio of just 0.16 percent, and the minimum initial investment is $3,000.

The next is the Fidelity Spartan 500 index (FUSEX). Because of its size, fidelity made sure that its indexing comes close to that of Vanguard and it is always second to that of vanguard as it offers the expense ratio of just 0.10 percent with the minimum initial investment which could be as low as $2,500. FUSEX holds the same stocks as VFINX, but the expense ratio is quite low.

Schwab S&P 500 Index is the next best index for the long term purpose. For Charles Schwab, he has been able to make that conscious effort to provide more than just discount brokerage services to investors, but he has been able to dig deep into the index funds markets of

Vanguard and Fidelity to bring out something good. In recent years, the discount broker has been able to lower the expenses just to compete for head to head with Vanguard and Fidelity. The expense ratio is as low as 0.09 percent, and the minimum initial investment is a ridiculous $100.

This chapter will be incomplete if we fail to mention the best aggressive stock index funds. As a long-term investor, you wouldn't mind seeing market fluctuations and your account balance just going up and down in a very short period right? So, you'll find aggressive stock index funds very attractive.

Vanguard Growth Index (VIGRX) is the first on this list. This fund invests only in the large cap stocks which have growth potential. Although it is a bit risky, it has much potential rewards and winnings in the long run than even the S&P 500 index funds. The expense ratio is 0.22%, and the minimum initial investment is $3,000.

Fidelity NASDAQ Composite Index (FNCMX). This index like the Vanguard growth consists of fat, large-cap stocks which would give you a greater long-term growth potential than the broad market indices. If the added risk is okay for this long-term return potential, you'll be attracted to the FNCMX which has a ratio of 0.29 percent and a minimum initial investment of $2500.

For the best Bond Index Funds, there are two major options which fall under the bracket of index funds we've been using for a while now. The Vanguard Total Bond Market Index (VBMFX) and the Fidelity Total Bond (FTBFX) also. The Vanguard has an expense ratio of 0.16 percent, and that minimum initial investment is $3,000 while that of fidelity is a 0.45 percent expense ratio and a $2500 minimum initial purchase.

Financial Freedom

Have you ever felt trapped in a Rat Race and wished you could retire quickly with enough money in your bank account? You must have felt that you are spending way too much than you are earning, right?

Have you ever felt that you are only helping your boss to get the life that you want or deserve? Have you ever felt that you are spending most of your life building the dreams of others and not yours? Well, that feeling is mutual. Sometimes in the past, I felt frustrated because I was deep in debt, I thought I wouldn't be able to retire because I felt that as soon as I do so, the money will stop coming and thus I wouldn't be able to pay off my mortgages and credit card. We feel trapped because there are too many bills to pay, too many dreams to fulfill and it seems as if we have little or no time. Take a few moments to think of the reason why you work. If your answer is to make money, then I am afraid that you are still caught up in that rat race. Most individuals would tie themselves to the shackles of their job and debt because they feel there is no way of escape.

You have a choice!

You have that liberty to decide when you want to work, without thinking of your boss or thinking that your career is at stake. In fact, you'll have that freedom to go on that vacation you so much desire troubles of retrenchments thereafter. There is nothing as good as freedom. I can tell you that. I am sure you really crave for financial freedom, if not you wouldn't be reading this book right now. How do you think you can be free financially? Are you getting a better job with a higher paycheck? I am sorry to disappoint you, but that wouldn't work. When you have high paychecks you would be thinking of an expensive lifestyle right, and even more, responsibilities would begin to come your way, then you begin to work more hours. It all leads back to the same circle.

If you can get a good grip on this, you would be exposed to the fact that financial freedom is not measured by how long you are working. You don't work hard. You work smart. Consequently, financial freedom is definitely not about amazing abundant riches or getting that golden lifestyle.

Now, you may think that there is nothing like financial freedom. And craving for financial freedom isn't realistic. Well, that's just your feelings. Financial freedom is possible. It is important for you to know now that ordinary people have achieved financial freedom if you think you have to be as rich as Bill Gates, Jeff Bezos, Jack Ma or Oprah Winfrey before you achieve it, you are probably having the wrong line of thought.

Before we think of financial freedom, first is financial freedom a reality?

As I have mentioned earlier, if you think financial freedom is unrealistic, please save yourself the time and effort by dropping this book. But if you want to achieve financial freedom and you believe that it is possible to be free from the rat race, then immerse all the contents in this book and make sure you practice them. Financial freedom is not an impossible fantasy.

All of us dream of financial freedom; however many of us think that it is just something in the abstract or some kind of fantasy. Most times we think about it from time to time, sigh and forget it. We do this because we have that believe that a state as good as financial freedom is only reserved for millionaires in the world. Can this freedom ever be a reality? Even when we accept that it is a reality, we think it only applies to the super-rich.

Nonetheless, the truth remains that financial freedom cannot be possible with this kind of mental attitude. If you want to be financially free, you have to believe that it is possible to be financially free. Next, you need to build your confidence. You have to be confident that anyone, yes, anyone can be financially free, provided that he/she is willing to work towards it. If you fail to have this positive attitude, you are never going to make it. So the very first step would be to fine-tune your mentality and believe in it from your inside. You can design your life the way you prefer it all depends on you. Now you may be thinking; *why is he telling me to believe in something I know little or nothing about.* The truth remains that if you take this book and read it passively if you fail to put the information into use, you probably didn't believe in financial freedom. You may decide that you may want to gain financial freedom by starting your own business. What should you do? Have a vision for it. Think of a business that no one has thought of before. Is this possible? Yes, it is. And it starts by believing in yourself, trusting yourself that you can do it. Even if your idea exists, you should execute it differently. Execution is what makes you different from your competitors. There is no point in starting something for financial security and having no faith in it. If you do not earn enough money to support your dream of being a financially free person, then you need to find means of making money to make such dreams come true.

I would try to make this as quickly as possible — a short story of how I became financially independent in 5 years. Note; I am not a very close relative of Gate's or brother to Mark. I am as ordinary as you could think I am. However, this isn't a formula. So don't think you have to follow the details of what I did to reach a similar goal. When I began my journey towards financial freedom, I didn't consider it as a journey to financial freedom. I just had that goal that I wanted to do things differently, and I wanted to go faster — 3-4 years instead of 5. I wanted to make a six-figure income. The truth remains that as we gain in knowledge and wisdom, our priorities change from what seems to be less important to bigger perspectives having pivotal goals. First of all, we need to get some things straight about me. I have never been dumb with money. I have never been in the red zone. And please note that I am not saying this to feel good about myself. But just to let you know that most times, you are born with some innate qualities which give you "an upper hand" over others. At a point in my life, I realized that my expensive hobbies had to go and be replaced with "free" hobbies. Most times, I would save to buy a computer, then an SLR camera, then a HiFi rack then I would save to get another computer, then a telescope. It took me time to make the connection between hobbies and things that can get me money.

Somehow, I got influenced by two personal finance books; one of which we all know *Rich Dad Poor Dad* and *Your money or your life*. I learned how to calculate my real wage by subtracting taxes, transport, business clothes, cost of living, etc. from the later. The Rich Dad Poor Dad standard made me think like a poor person and save and pay in cash. I was probably on the way to think like a middle-class person who buys everything on credit. What weighs down the middle class is a large set of liabilities in the form of house payments, car payments, credit payments, educational payments, etc. Having these liabilities make it hard for you to replace them with assets.

At first, I started by just putting my money in savings accounts and watch them grow. But what seems to be very key here is that I did not start investing for the first 3 years out of the 6 years it took me to gain financial freedom. Another thing I noticed early is those small expenditures added up quickly. $10 there, $100 there, $50 there, $5 every day for the month and you wouldn't know when you have little or nothing to save. In months were I bought very little my savings seemed to go up very fast. I tapped into the provision of opportunity cost. I found out that you don't need to spend a lot of money to be *comfortable.*

Furthermore, I made my lifestyle as simple as possible. I relied more on skills and adaptation to the environment rather than thinking of money. As funny as it sounds, I began looking for substitutes for shampoo or toothpaste. I even knew how to make baking soda! I could cook with almost no heat and very few utensils. What was I driving at? Budgeting, budgeting, and budgeting. I had to cut the cost of living drastically. Apart from budgeting, I wanted to make everything I truly needed to live well fit into a couple of large suitcases and reduce my expenditures to what is considered somewhat below the poverty level while I maintained a comfortable lifestyle.

When I got my Ph.D., I had no student debt. I became an academic researcher, and I was about making as much as a state trooper or a long haul trucker. I still searched for creative ways to save money. More also having just graduated with a Ph.D. and paired everything I could possibly need into a couple of large suitcases. I moved to my new job with everything in a couple of suitcases. Before my arrival, I had decided that after 4 years of sharing a kitchen and bathroom with over 15 other people, I wanted the luxury of my own kitchen and my own bathroom. I was so lucky to find a room on top of a house which the Landlord rented to students and researchers. It was within walking distance of my new job, so I was good to go. The only problem I had was how to move my bank accounts. So after a week of eating out with my new boss, etc. I was down to a couple of cans of tuna, a large bag of rice, and some soy sauce for the second week until I got my paycheck.

Because I was able to cut all my expenses to the bare essentials, I was able to save approximately 60-90% of my net income through grad school and my subsequent jobs with an average percentage in the mid-eighties. At first, this money went directly to my savings account. I fumbled early into investing early. When I say this most people ask about it so here it goes.

At the end of 2005, I was getting tired of earning just 1.5% in my savings accounts. I needed more. Since I grew up in a country where investing in stocks was considered too speculative I started to do my personal research. I called my bank and told them that I wanted to buy some bonds. I have directed to some Baa-rated something bonds. It was a company which finances ships at 3%, and I put down $20,000 at 3%. I was earning $600 a year. I needed something doing so I made a program to predict my net worth. I would type in my assets, and the return on investment (ROI) would appear coupled along with my monthly contribution. This process would calculate my net worth for the next 80 years. I put in statements like "if this" then "this" "if that" then this, "financial independence reached at 4% withdrawal", "my first million," "and my second million" etc. I ran this program twice a day, and I knew my net worth down to the cent. Then I was a young and enthusiastic person, pretty much ignorant about anything investment or business. I was completely clueless. But I remembered that I had much interest in geopolitics and demographic trends. I called my broker once more and told him I wanted to buy some stock in a company producing insulin (because people were getting older and fatter) I also telephoned a telephone company, wind power company, and a small cap holding company. Later I also got an airline company too. You see serious danger right? But as it happened, most positions turned out to perform well except for the airline. I was getting returns of 30% a year. I sold the airline and the wind company too. The funny thing is that today, I wish I had put all my money in those stocks and not just the fraction I did then. (about $40,000). Making these investments drastically increased my ROI. And in my program, I also had an average estimated monthly investment income as well as my average monthly expenses. My investment story turns out to be very complicated by the fact that I was learning more rapidly than the market. Within a year I started pulling money out of the funds to begin a broker account. I read tons of 400 pages of books on how to manipulate the return structure of your investment.

My math geeks may want to consider this. You can skip this paragraph if you find it complex. I am just using this instance, examples, and stories to tell you that being financially free isn't something abstract. Saving 70-80% means spending only 20-30% right? Really small? Well if expenses can be covered by extracting 4% from savings and investments annually, one needs to save a total of 20-

30%/0.04=500-750%. Without adding the compound interest etc. this would take 500/80=6.25 years or 750/70=10.7 years. What are the two important conclusions here? One, the 10% difference between 70% and 80% makes a big difference in the estimated time which takes to gain financial freedom. Second, compound interest will only play a minor role. It can move the retirement date to 4 or5 years instead of 6 years. The standard recommended 15% savings rate results in 25 years. This result isn't a coincidence as this is very comparable to the time most people spend working before they retire. Having a long time compound interest doesn't make any difference.

Like you know, things have changed a lot since I started. I recalled celebrating when my first investment went up by $2-"Like a babe, I earned $2 on the stock market today!" but nowadays my portfolio fluctuates sometimes by a paycheck on a daily basis. Gaining or losing our digit figures is not a big deal anymore. "Oh, babe by the way I lost/made $5,000 last week." I still sleep well at night.

How do I look at myself today? "Me, Inc." instead of "Who Cares, Inc." What my day job does is to generate a consistent alpha that is a time-based performance. However, must of my income is beta (market-based). I take control of my own investments, and this has turn into investing into a second job for me. In fact, I can earn more managing my investments than I could, taking on a second (minimum wage) job. This is why I presently, I don't need a "real job."

If I can do this, you can do much more. Financial freedom is not a myth. It has never been, and it could never be. My long and boring story has been able to show you that you need first to believe in yourself, believe in your plan, work out that plan which includes taking action, stay with it, develop yourself and watch how freedom becomes a reality.

I would want you to look at financial freedom has not having to work anymore in order to live, because your money will be working harder than you do. It will pay your bills, your food, and even your play. The earlier you get there. Almost everyone wants to be financially free. That definition of financial freedom is very true; in fact, 100% true. However, that's not all about financial freedom. Yes, you have money, "somuch" money that you don't need to work but have you ever felt so empty because you are idle. We crave for financial freedom, but some of us find it hard to stay unoccupied. Financial freedom is managing your time and making the best of it.

In the process of becoming financially free, there are several stumbling blocks along the way which you have to overcome. These stumbling blocks are called; Financial Hurdle. One of my favorite quotes from Manoj Arora's *From the Rat Race to Financial Freedom* talks about being different and achieving what the extraordinary can only dare to do. *To achieve what 1% of the world's population have (Financial Freedom), you must be willing to do what only 1% dare to do. Hard work and perseverance of highest order.*

This takes us to the first obstacle to financial freedom. YOU! Yes, you. You can be your own stumbling block. *You are only as rich as your willpower-* Wayne Chirisa. Most times we wait when we suppose to move and spend when we are expected to invest. You need to overcome every fear, every unbelief. Personally, you can be an obstacle to yourself if you lack the following things:

- Education: Sadly, your salary has no manual like those appliances you buy. There is no operation manual on how you spend the money you earn. So most times you end up not budgeting or spending more than you can afford and not investing. The soonest you can educate yourself, the better you will be in the position to do something about your financial servitude. Now education is not about going to school. Just because I mentioned obtaining my Ph.D. in the previous chapter doesn't mean that I am *highly* educated. Education is applying that wealth of knowledge acquired by the individual study of a particular subject matter or experiencing life lessons that provide an understanding of something. It is way beyond four walls of a school. To be able to become financially free, Education is the best defense and Action is the best offense- Dr. Pinky Intal

- Action but have education: Yes, you may know what to do, but you have a fear of taking that leap. Educating yourself without action is meaningless. A total waste of time.

Just as I have mentioned earlier in the book, you should read with an open mind. The next few points I would give now may surprise you. The truth is bittersweet. Take it, think about it and channel your life towards it.

Another personal hurdle may be your parents or close relative. Does it sound surprising? However, not all parents or close relatives are created equal. You should know that some become your ally and support you while others become obstacles of your dream to be financially free. Being a financial consultant for years, I have been able to observe that there are big factors in making financial decisions and the source of these decisions are as important as the decision itself. If you have parents born in the mid-'90s, they are probably not open to things like insurance, investment for retirement, etc. Most people who are not adaptto changing often oppose them. Nevertheless, if you are already at your right age, you have that freedom to make the decision yourself. You combine education with your freedom of choice. With that, you can never go wrong. Matthew B. Brock, CFP says; *Generation Y is constantly being told that there is a right way to plan financially. This advice often comes from an older generation whose financial status doesn't show that their way is the right way.* Being financially free also requires some level of freedom. Mental freedom.

Your spouse could be an obstacle to financial freedom. Actually, what she doesn't know would hurt you. The same applies to you. What you don't know would hurt her. If you spend time investing in yourself, educating yourself financially but your spouse remains ignorant, he/she can put both of you down. Definitely, in every financial decision, it remains important for you to be honest with your spouse. Where the problem lies is when you wanted to act, and she fails to go along with you, the family suffers for it. When seeking advice from financial experts, you don't go alone. Go with your spouse. Make sure both of you are present there so that you can be educated together on the best decision to take for your family.

Let me share a true story here.

Kimberly and Blake are married with 5 children. Blake works as a seaman; Kimberly takes care of their kids. One day, he met Sarah (a financial expert). As a financial expert Sarah suggested, he gets life insurance to be able to establish a good financial foundation first before they even invest. Since he is the only breadwinner and he got lots of dependents. Blake told Kimberly, but Kimberly declines. What she wanted was more savings so that they could go to Manila as vacation and besides, she reasoned that Blake has life insurance coverage as a seaman. The premium on life insurance is like an added expense to her. Then the unexpected happens, while Blake is in the Philippines for vacation, he met a tragic car accident which killed him. The life insurance policy as a seaman is not applicable. Kimberly has to work now to support his 5 children. In the end, the wife's wrong choice took them both away from their children. Blake, dying without leaving anything to their children and Kimberly as a mother now need to work night and day to support her kids. She ended up leaving their children to relatives.

A tragic story right? This happens all the time though. Let me end this point with this: *Wives from time to time object to Life Insurance. . . Widows Never Do!*

The norm of the society can also come as a stumbling block to financial freedom. What do we do now? We buy the latest gadget, travel to different places, have luxurious celebrations, etc. These things aren't bad at all. But when you see your friends having these, the desire to have them for yourself intensifies. Truth be told, lifestyle upgrade isn't a bad idea. But before you think of upgrading your lifestyle make sure you already have the proper financial foundation in place. Make sure you have it laid down for you. The basic needs for you and your family should be present. You should be sure that you have gotten yourself out of every debt, you have saved up for emergencies, and you have insured your income with life insurance. *If you keep needing what you want, there will come a time you will want what you really need-* Ricky So.

This chapter will be incomplete if we fail to mention the four biggest emotions and mindset blocks which stand in the way of taking and action and succeeding with our financial goals.

- ✓ Having a comfort zone: A comfort zone is one of the biggest challenges you would have to overcome if you have one. The only way you can change your financial life for good is to start being comfortable with feeling uncomfortable. The wealthy are aware of this. They know that evolving and growing comfort zone is key to success. You become very capable of dealing with fear the moment comfort becomes a big factor in your life. Don't be angry that you don't have money now, don't be frustrated that you can't get your wants. Let that feeling push you to make that success move.

✓ Doubt: The rich and the poor have an equal share of this. What makes the difference is what you are able to do, the decision you are able to take even when you are faced with doubt. The solution to acting despite your doubt is understanding that variety is another way to view uncertainty. When doubt comes, don't retreat to your comfort zone. Move forward, seek new opportunities and possibilities.

✓ Worry: I once heard this statement from someone; *the rich worry a lot because they have stocks everywhere.* Well, I don't know how true that is based on the next point below. I think it may be so. But wouldn't you rather worry in your own mansion or penthouse than to worriless in a rented apartment? Dealing with your finances can cause a lot of worries. We stress about having enough, making more money, losing money, and we also worry about taxes, business ideas, and profits, investments, etc. How can you deal with the stress that follows? Take action! Keep taking action.

✓ Inconvenience: We really need to face the fact here. Sometimes, being rich is not always going to be convenient. And it wouldn't be easy also. Much effort than you think is needed to change your financial status. Life will always be hard but you should be willing to take the hard road, and things would become easy. Get out of that comfort zone, make hard choices. It isn't going to be easy. But I tell you that every inch of discomfort you experience would be replaced with numerous satisfaction as time goes on.

No-one is free from the financial rat race. Even professionals who are up in their game are gaining a lot at the end of the month. They also face some obstacles.

First, they are isolated because people feel that they don't *need help*. The truth remains that it is hard to build wealth on your own. You are vulnerable alone, and you may never reach your fullest potential when you are not with the right people. In today's changing financial environment it's very pivotal than ever before to have the support of a mastermind group. They are also worn-out by fear like others also. They are faced with the fear of failure (a very prevalent one), fear of debt, fear of success and fear of the unknown.

The choice is yours. Below, I have listed four financial categories you currently fall into. However, it left to you to decide today about which category you want to work towards achieving.

1. Financial Crisis:

You have no savings

Live from mouth to mouth

Spend more than you earn.

Consistently rely on credit to get through.

Have more than two credit cards and use one to pay the other.

2. Financial stability:

You live within your means.

You have sufficient savings to cover for three months of your basic living expenses which include mortgage/rent, car, debts, rates, water, insurance, utilities, and food.

Three months is measured stability because that is how long it takes the average person to find another job if they lose theirs. If you go with the thought that it may take more than 3 months to secure a job, then you would have to increase the amount of months savings to match.

3. Financial Security:

You have sufficient savings or capital invested (i.e., property and/or shares) to provide you an annual income to cover 12 months of your basic living expenses.

4. Financial Freedom/ independence:

This is when you have financial capital invested to the extent that you can survive without ever having to work again. You have an infinite income which allows you to live your dreams without limitations and you can afford to get something without asking *"how much is that?"*

The choice is yours; Face the hurdles of financial restraints now, overcome them, stick to your plan, make sure you achieve them. Then sit back, relax, enjoy your retirement and live a stress-free life.

Paths To Financial Freedom

So you must have made that decision to take control of your financial future and freedom. Or are you yet to do that? But how are you supposed to achieve this? Especially with countless promises and products which guarantee your success. It becomes very easy for you to give up even without starting. Just take your time to go to the search engine and type in make money from home or make money online. You would be bombarded with some get rich quick schemes with fake promises. Is there any way to be financially free? Do we have any path to financial independence?

We should start first by having the mentality of the rich. Research has it that the most influential part of one's life is between ages 4 and 18. Between these age brackets, we become exposed to information we will ever use as a person. Printed in our hearts and minds are the guidelines of how the world works, how we can make our futures and the right way to live for everyone or most people. You are taught how to work hard, get things done by yourself and interact with other people doing the same thing. You become rooted in the rat race as you are thought how to be a successful employee for the rest of your life.

The idea of being a good employee is not a bad idea. But definitely, it is not a path of victory or conquest. Sure that feeling that people get when they land the job they want or get that promotion they've been waiting for is incomparable. However, when you become an employee, you become tied to this never-ending ladder full of steps for you to climb. You will be very happy when everything comes together for you every few years. You go to work for a few more years to feel good. Then eventually you are given the honor to retire, take a pay cut, and live off a small salary until you die. The number one path to financial freedom is to hate your job. Yes! Hate it. Don't be satisfied with it. Tell me isn't it boring. Getting up each day, going to work, coming back, it sounds monotonous.

Your financial freedom comes when you are able to save, invest money wisely and accumulate assets for the future through carefully planned strategies. Paths to financial freedom include; planning, gaining financial knowledge, having the discipline to practice things that need to be done and believing in yourself. Just as I have mentioned earlier your desire to achieve financial freedom is the generating power of ACTION. Success will only come if you do something you believe in.

First, you have to set your financial goals. Your financial goals like every other goal can be classified as Short term, midterm, and Long term. Make sure your goals are realistic. You should learn to treat yourself as a business manager, responsible for managing your financial resources. To be successful financially, you really need to know where you are going and how you will get there. Setting goals are as important as deciding to be financially free. You need to be able to transform these ideas and dreams into reality. You can't just sit back and hope the money will fall from the sky (although that would be nice!) Take time to strategize for the future. A realistic goal is a goal which can be measured. You must be able to say that at this time, I should have $20,000 in my account.

In addition to the above, you should develop your own personal money management program. Well, how can you do this? Educate yourself. Read books, try schemes. Meet with other professionals, financial planners, and banks. When developing your personal money management program, you are expected to live within your income. Know how much you spend, your financial responsibilities and how to control expenses.

Next, you develop an effective savings plan. Your savings objectives will be dependent on your current economic circumstances. The world's most financially successful people make saving a priority. Just putting away the smallest amount of money each month into your savings account can perform wonders for you and your family. This habit of continuously investing in savings to build wealth over time have been practiced by most of the successful people in the world. When you plan your savings, you stop impulsive buying drastically. We all know that feeling of buying something on a whim. It is exciting, and it leaves us wanting for more. The culture of mass consumption has made most of us fall victim of the temptation of buying impulsively and making unplanned purchases. Behavior like this is very dangerous for our bank accounts. Sadly, we know this, but we still fall into that trap. People that are financially stable plan their purchases weigh the pros and cons of all their buying decisions.

Another thing is to learn to invest wisely. Your goal is to increase your wealth over time and to get the best possible return from the money you invest. It is important for you here to always take into account the prevailing economy. Each type of investment comes with its level of risk and consequences. You should understand this properly. You should read and analyze all documents given to you in the bank and all the fine print before signing anything and, only after you have sought professional help. Furthermore, you may want to consider if the investment is suitable for you or whether it is the right time to invest. You should also think of how much you can safely afford to invest? The benefits and risk involved. Will the investment provide a reasonable return for the amount of money invested? You should also consider; your assets and liabilities, current interest rates and cost involved. Nevertheless, you should consider the following:

- Your assets and liabilities
- Current interest rates and the costs involved
- Fully understanding the benefits and the consequences of effective credit use.
- Investigate all sources and always look for the best deals. This means that you shouldn't be satisfied with what you are getting from your stockbroker. There is nothing bad in seeking advice from multiple stockbrokers.
- Make sure you deal with well-established firms and qualified people
- Never be late in repaying loans.

It would be so unprofessional of me to conclude this chapter without making mention of the online aspect of financial freedom and how you can be able to tap into this resource. Not in this day where we have Bitcoin Millionaires and the like. Many individuals have created financial freedom through building business offline and the traditional way, like opening up a retail store, or buying real estate, selling insurance the list really goes on to infinite ways it has been done before. But the reality remains stagnant. You can start a virtual online empire which will skyrocket you to financial freedom faster than any of the traditional means you know. Most people have bad taste in their mouth when they hear anything online like network marketing because of all the failure stories they hear. The truth remains that they are just stories. Most times people fail in this industry because they do not stick with it long enough to see that it works.You are sticking with the plan. Remember? You must have that resilience to remain through the good and bad times in order to prosper. And this goes for every kind of business you may want to venture into. When it comes to having an online business empire, first you must be able to keep up with technology and have a real mentor to teach you. Definitely, you will hit bumps on the road to success, but that is not a good reason for you to give up on your dreams and goals.

Today, more millionaires are coming out of the network marketing industry today than any other industry you have out there. You are the only one who can make the decision to achieve financial freedom. Get yourself familiarized with your *computer*.The computer here doesn't necessarily mean the device. But any instrument you intend to use, phones, applications, bitcoin, etc. Furthermore, you need to take calculated risk also. With just a click you can lose millions and gain millions too. Think of this as a chess game. You make specific moves to keep away from the checkmate. The wiser your decisions are and the faster you take action, the faster you will achieve financial freedom.

I would highlight some practical paths to success and how to get started. Don't look at this as a repeat of the points above but rather a reinforcement. In mapping out your financial freedom path, you must be:

- Be accountable and responsible: The very step on the path of financial success is for you to accept responsibility. Only you are in control of your financial future, and every choice you make would definitely havean impact. Irrespective of your age, education or background. You need to ask yourself questions that matter; are you completing your own financial aid paperwork? Are you in charge or do you have equal input in paying your bills and managing your finances? Do you do thorough research before you make any big purchase (like a car or computer)? When you become involved from the start, you become aware of your responsibilities and obligations. You also need to ask yourself these questions; if you lend money or enter into another financial commitment, do you always understand your rights and responsibilities? Are the *terms* and *conditions* gibberish? Do you find business news boring?

Being responsible also involves paying your debts on time. When you pay late, do you know it has a great effect on you? You know that the credit bureaus are always quick to compile your report and also calculate your score. When you pay late, your credit score drops. This credit score is usually based on; how you pay bills on time, the total amount of debt you have and how close to your credit limit that amount is, the number of accounts you recently opened, the number of recent inquiries about your credit score, the different type of accounts currently opened, the length of time you have been building credit. Your creditors will grade you on these and even more. Therefore, put off the coat of irresponsibility, carelessness, and sloppiness now!

- Plot your course of action: This is where I remind you that you have to be specific, being specific isn't the only thing, but you also need to be realistic. Most importantly you need to WRITE DOWN YOUR GOALS. When you write down your goals, you would be able to keep records and mark off key milestones as you achieve them. When you review your goals, and you record your progress, you motivate yourself. After you have been able to identify your goals, you map out how you are going to achieve them. Several questions are needed to be answered; like how much income do you have available? How much will you need to achieve your goal (this is where you have to be as realistic as possible)? Do you have any other goal you need to finish before you start planning? Financial freedom is a journey where you'll need total focus.

- Understand your income: Let's picture this. You've just been offered a job at a local firm. They've offered you 40 hours per week starting from $15 per hour; this means that you'll be taking home $600 (40X15) dollars a week right?

Wrong!

If you have no understanding of your income, I advise that you get that report, document or anything you need to get from your employee.

In understanding your income, you need to know that there are numerous deductions take from your gross pay (the hours multiplied by your hourly wage). What you receive after all these deductions have been made is the net pay. Standard deductions are; federal income tax, social security, and Medicare. Other deductions include: state taxes, additional retirement contributions, health insurance, cafeteria plan benefits, wage garnishment, agreed automatic withholdings, etc. Note that all these charges are individually distinct.

- Open a checking account: What does a checking account do? Why do I have to open it? It should be noted that this point is just a suggestion, just like every other thing in this book. It must not be taken hook line and sinker. A checking account is a very secure place to keep your money. Not that all other accounts are less secure, but it helps you track your money. What a checking account does is that it creates a paper trail which would help you in knowing how much money is available to spend and how much you have spent. But before you open a checking account, you must do thorough research to find a bank or credit union which provides an account which suits your needs. And just as I have mentioned. If you don't know everything about it, don't go into it. We

have three common types of account;
the standard, special and interest-
bearing account. We have some special
banks which offer "free" checking
accounts and other enticements
specifically for students, etc. The check
register is also an important element in
your checking account. You should
record all transaction, deposit,
withdrawals, deduction, etc. For
example, you have; cash deposit-the
checks are written, ATM or debit card
transactions should also be monitored.

- Start saving and investing money. If you
  don't have a savings account, I would
  advise that you should open one now! I
  should also emphasize here that you
  should pay yourself first! Depositing
  money into a savings account should
  take priority over any additional
  spending. As you pay your monthly
  bills, make sure to set money aside to

deposit into your savings. You can also ask your bank to automatically transfer money from your checking to your savings once, twice or thrice a month. You can also request a direct deposit from your employer for a portion of your paycheck to be deposited into your savings.

- Borrow smart: Whenever you are considering taking any loan. You should consider; the interest rate, additional fees, and down payments. However, there are some additional guidelines to help you determine whether or not to borrow money; first, housing expenses should not exceed 33 percent of what you have as gross income. A lot of lending institutions look at this factor in determining your loan eligibility. Furthermore, loan installment payments which include auto and student loans, as well as credit cards, should not exceed a combined total of 20 percent of what appears to be your gross income. Finally, save money and have at least 6-12 months of emergency savings.

Finance gurus, stock brokers, employees, and even employers keep talking about becoming financially free. However, the truth remains that if you want to become financially free, you must be ready to take passive income as serious as the major source of income. I know this may sound too serious, but that is the truth. Passive income is not really passive; it is a serious aspect of your financial life that you should give all attention also.

There are four major sources which can serve as that extra well of passive income.

✓ The Earned income. This is the money earned from your time and energy. People have those side hustle which helps them get some extra income.

✓ The portfolio income is the kind of income you receive from extra dividends and capital gains which comes from owning stocks and other mutual funds.

✓ Leverage income is generated when one particular occupation or pursuit gives you more money larger than that captured audience. Let's take for example you plan to give a lecture to 200 people, but only 20 arrive, you stock their heads with so many principles that they demand other things (materials) meant for the 200. You've earned much with the smaller group.

✓ You may want to consider passive income as this side hustle which involves investment, and it produces cash like every other business transaction

We can definitely tell from the above that earned incomes puts you in the position to pay your bills, but it would also sustain you until you're able to get such promotions and raises. That is why you shouldn't limit your income by just putting all your eggs in one basket.

So with passive income, you would be able to create that compound flow of income. Increase your passive income, and you'll be able to lift yourself out of every financial problem to become financially free.

The following are some suggestions on how you can begin to make some passive income.

- License a patent
- Cash flow positive real estate
- Automated fulfillment websites
- Pay for use items
- Build a successful business
- Become an Author: Copyrighting materials that earn royalties, such as books or e-books, especially is a strong

way entrepreneurs create passive income.

- We should know that passive income does not necessarily mean that there is no involvement on your end. Creating passive income streams often involves a large investment up-front, but in the end, it requires little or no interaction.

- Also, just because you make an earned income now (opposed to passive income) does not mean that you should quit your day job and open up a quarter car wash. To start building passive income streams, you will likely need to keep making an earned income in order to convert that income into passive income by purchasing rental properties, etc. Active income can actually be extremely beneficial in creating more passive income.

- Once your passive income is greater than your expenses, you can make the decision to stop making an earned income and live the rest of your life financially free.

Conclusion

Thank you for reading this book and I really hope you enjoyed it and have learnt that anybody can use the stock market amongst other things to become financially free and finally be free of the burden that is debt. While it may seem I am against active investing, I am certainly not and I do myself invest in an active manner on top of my index funds. However, this requires much more work and research and if you are interested in taking that route I would highly recommend educating yourself further on active investing in the Stock Market with books, courses and potentially even a mentor. I personally have some books on active investing and am in the process of producing more. But, for the average person who doesn't want to dedicate hours and hours to research and education I wholeheartedly recommend index funds and passive investing as the easiest way to build a substantial nest egg for your retirement or early retirement if that is your goal.

Also, please remember the Stock Market is one way to build wealth, however, there are many more ways to also build wealth. For example starting a business and then reinvesting profits either back in the business or into the Stock Market and continuing to let it all compound over decades adds even more power to Compound Interest. I would recommend not becoming narrow minded and researching all the ways to build wealth whether that be through "Active" income, "Passive" income or investments such as the Stock Market and Real Estate. We live in an ever changing world so always be prepared to adapt. I don't imagine for one second that our grandparents believed they would be able to send a "text message" let alone video call anyone from anywhere in the world within seconds. The world is always changing and as individuals we need to be able to keep up with the ever changing world.

Anyways, I hope this book has opened your eyes to how lucrative the Stock Market can be and how simple investing can be with the power of index funds, passive investing and compound interest. Here's to your success!

Real Estate Investing

The Ultimate Practical Guide To Making your Riches, Retiring Early and Building Passive Income with Rental Properties, Flipping Houses, Commercial and Residential Real Estate

Table of Contents

Chapter One: Introduction

At the young age of 29, while others were buried in student debt and dead-end jobs, Kris Burns, a self-made real estate investor who started off with no capital funding now feels like he can breathe with ease and anticipate a bright future ahead. It has taken him four years to get to this position.

He's driving his dream car, traveling the world and has finally managed to hire a personal trainer to help him shed some of the extra weight that used to make him feel self-conscious. Best of all, the girl of his dreams just said yes, and they are planning a wedding for next fall. Life is beautiful in Kris's world.

But the path to this point hasn't been easy. Not too long ago he was crippled by student debt. He had a Masters degree, but no hope for a high paying flexible job and no money in the bank. This isn't a unique case.

Many well-educated men and women find themselves stuck in a life that feels like hell with no way out. Even if they are fortunate enough to get a well-paying job after university, they quickly realize a salary cannot lead to financial freedom. Sure, we hear of people making it big in today's society, but for the most part, the majority of our population is still struggling financially. As the cost of living increases and the marketplace shifts, thinking of the future can be very daunting. Unless you figure out a way (as Kris did) to create your own economy.

How did Kris go from struggle and no hope of financial prosperity to his dream lifestyle?

Simple. Kris found a way to turn himself into an investor in the Real Estate industry. He learned how to make money in his own way independent of a boss or a bank. After being a full-time Real Estate investor for the past four years, Kris is reaping the lavish benefits of his hard work in both active and passive income. When he started out, he had no money, poor credit scores, and no experience.

Perhaps very similar to where you might be now. By simply adhering to certain fundamental principles, the same ones you'll be learning in this book, and doing things in a certain way, he's now able to lead an affluent lifestyle. Kris knew life would never be the same again when one of his deals brought in 65,000 in profit and he experienced that first-time thrill of making more money in a few months than he'd ever made his entire life. From that point on, he went all in and has been reaping the benefits ever since. The same thing could happen for you if you only take this book and implement the secrets contained within.

What to expect from this book:

Real estate investing has always been considered a game for more prominent players in society. Those with cash and status often make it work for them. Andrew Carnegie said, "ninety percent of all millionaires become so through owning real estate. More money has been made in real estate than in all industrial investments combined. The wise young man or wage earner of today invests his money in real estate."

His words ring true even in this age of the Internet and technology. No one can deny the Internet has made it possible for us to create new income-producing channels, but at the end of the day, Real Estate is always going to be a no-brainer.

As long as human beings are civilized and living in houses, there will always be plenty of money to be made. Now let me ask you this:

Would you like to dip your toes into this lucrative industry and make money your own way?

Will you choose to take the wise words of Carnegie and become a man or woman who invests in Real Estates and makes millions?

If you answered yes, then this book will help you map out the journey of being a smart Real Estate Investor.

It doesn't matter how much experience or cash you have. Once you've made the decision that you must make this happen for you, implementing the strategies and tactics shared in this book will naturally yield results for you.

This book will teach you the fundamentals of Real Estate investing and how to make it the vehicle that helps you retire early and lead a wealthy lifestyle. As I said, you don't even need to have prior experience.

If you're a total beginner with little to no cash as well, this is unquestionably for you.

If you've always dreamed of becoming a millionaire in this lifetime, before you're too old to enjoy life, then this book is definitely for you. It will break down simple ways of starting out, how to find incredible deals, how to analyze those deals, finance them and create profitable exit strategies.

The education you need if you want financial freedom:

Although people like to make real estate elusive and confusing, I can assure you, it's not rocket science. Any man or woman can create significant success in real estate investing with proper planning and execution. Before that can become a reality for you, however, you need to recognize the importance of getting the right education. Your education becomes the first step up the ladder of real estate success.

Without the right education, your ability to navigate the real estate market becomes mitigated and constricted. Whether you're a novice or a seasoned real estate investor education will always play an integral part in your business success. Statistics show that many people involved in real estate fail to achieve financial independence throughout their investment career (even though this is one of the safest forms of investments), not because they lack money but because they lack the right knowledge to do the right thing.

To succeed as a real estate investor you must be resourceful no doubt, but you also need the right knowledge. You must acquire the information that can help you become a better investor. Information that will enable you to know which choice is right for you and your clients.

As our digital economy morphs the real estate industry, it is becoming more than just "land investments." It's now expanded into an information exchange as well. Your customer holds the primary power, and they have access to the Internet. At any given point, these clients are using the Internet to acquire information. In fact, by the end of 2015, it was found that ninety-two percent of clients are doing web searches for shopping for a home and forty-two percent of clients believe that virtual tours do play a decisive role in purchasing a property.

People are finding their dream home through online searches now, and by the time you encounter a buyer, unless they live in a cave with no cellphone and Wi-Fi coverage, they've probably Goggled their problem first. Which means the best way for you to secure a deal is to be as informed as possible about your market. Information and a good strategy are critical. Your clients will trust you more when they find that you are an honest, trustworthy, knowledgeable and resourceful person. So before you downplay the importance of diligently going through this book or the importance of taking an excellent online course on real estate, do some homework on the current state of the marketplace and what it takes to succeed in today's digitally connected world. Money alone will not bring you the success and financial freedom you desire as a real estate investor.

How to use this book:

Unfortunately, the world of Real Estate investing is often overwhelming and confusing for the average person. Without proper education, it's likely you'll burn out and burn through your cash quicker than a gambling addict in Las Vegas. The purpose of this book is to help you avoid the common pitfalls of Real Estate investing. It outlines for you the fundamentals, so you can finally get ahead in life.

No longer will you need to feel as if you have to risk everything with your investments. Instead, I'll walk you through every strategy to find the right one that's right for you and the quality of life you wish to have. The best way to get the most out of this book is to take it a chapter at a time and implement on each section of the roadmap provided. Don't treat this as entertainment or motivation. Make things practical for yourself. Commit to taking action with every gained lesson, and you will come out a winner in this economy.

Whether you want to get started with Rental Properties, flipping houses, house hacking, student rentals or Wholesaling I've got you covered.

Some of what you'll learn includes:

•Why Real Estate is the key to early retirement and financial freedom.

•What the wealthiest men in the world know about Real Estate that you don't.

•The basics you need to know to make Real Estate work for you.

•How to minimize your risk as you start doing Real Estate deals.

•The difference between traditional Real Estate and the new innovative ways that people are leveraging today.

•The best Niches and strategies that you can dive into even as a beginner.

•The financial side of Real Estate and how to stay on top of the game.

•The secret to buying properties without any money.

And that's not all.

By the time you're done reading this book, not only will you know the math needed to succeed in this game, but you'll also have the confidence to go search for your next deal. So whether you've dabbled in this before or not, I encourage you to trust in this process and go through each chapter with an open mind ready to implement what you learn.

Let's get started.

Chapter 02: Why Real Estate Is The Key To Early Retirement And Financial Freedom

Is the idea of early retirement appealing to you?

And by early retirement, I don't just mean spending the rest of your days lazily chilling on the beach sipping piña coladas (although you can do that too if that's your dream). Instead what I mean is being in a position to work on projects you love at your own schedule, eliminating the need for a 9-to-5 and spending more time with the people you love. For most people, the dream is to be able to work a few hours a week and still make a great living.

If that's your dream, if you've always wanted to find financial freedom and a stable, safe source of income real estate investing is the perfect tool to get you there.

Think of this book like a beginners crash course meant to help you fast track the learning curve, offer insights on pitfalls to be aware of and provide guidance on best practices. With that comes the need to know which path of real estate investing is going to be lucrative. After all, who wants to put in all the effort, energy, and resources needed if there isn't enough of a reward to balance things out? Well, I can assure you, an abundant harvest awaits you if you choose to plant the right seeds at the right time and tend to them as any good farmer in the field.

Some of the benefits of investing in real estate versus stock or bonds:

At the core of any investment is the income that can be generated. Real estate guarantees a healthy income stream for you if you know what you're doing. It's a dependable monthly income that you can rely on regardless of economic fluctuations.

Even if you own rentals that aren't doing so well, chances are you'll be making more reliable income than someone who has invested in other assets like stocks or bonds. That doesn't mean stock investment is a bad idea, it just means if you want something safe that is sure to appreciate over time, and if you don't like drama and the suspense of market flops, then real estate is the better option. If you invest in a low-cost index fund of the entire stock market, you're probably going to create enormous wealth in the long run, but when first starting out, real estate is more advantageous in comparison to other passive investments.

For early retirees, it matters even more because real estate investing gets you steady income immediately whereas much of the game in stocks and bonds requires you never to touch it.

Real estate gives you more control over your money, how quickly you grow and the deals you invest in. Your skills and hustle become your best assets when you get into Real Estate investing. And if like so many people you lack cash for funding, your people skills become even more valuable. With a real estate deal, you can significantly improve a property and increase its rent and perceived value. And when you're also the one managing the properties well on the backend, that income stream remains under your control for years to come.

Take the example of an index fund again. Can you really control it?

Not quite. You can control when to buy, reinvent your dividends and when to sell it. End of story. The managers and employees of the companies you buy have more control over your success and income than you do.

There is no right or wrong in either of these options. But personally, it feels better when I know I can influence and control my investments.

Another added benefit of investing in real estate is timing. Real estate investing gives us something most passive index investments can't. The ability to time my wealth building efforts.

As someone with big dreams of financial freedom and early retirement, I'm guessing you've done your goal setting, and there's a due date you set for yourself. The only way to ensure your investments are growing and helping you reach that goal on time is by investing in the right things that are guaranteed to increase over a specific period. Preferably sooner rather than later.

With investments like stock indexes, growth can be extremely volatile over the short run. You always feel at the mercy of the stock prices, and if there should ever be a sudden dip or drop in stock prices, you can kiss your due date goodbye. No chance of financial independence if the stock prices act up. This has been experienced a lot recently with

Bitcoin and crypto-currency. It's a great game but a highly volatile one that's better suited for people who enjoy the drama and thrill of being in a never-ending roller coaster.

With real estate investing, however, you can breathe with ease because none of that drama and volatility applies. You have two very predictable growth options:

1. Positive rental income

2. Debt amortization (pay down)

Reliable rental income:

Although I'm not here to make ridiculous claims that cannot be backed up (and we all know any type of investments does require risk management), as a general rule, real estate has shown it can remain quite stable even during the worst times.

Take for example the housing crisis that hit some years ago. On the surface, it appeared as though things were going really bad, right? However, research issued by the U.S Census Bureau on January 30, 2018, surveying current population and housing vacancy during the recession years as well as before that shows that even at the worst times in the market (2008-2010), rents still remained stable or only experienced a slight decrease in most U.S markets. Of course, everything else including housing prices themselves plummeted.

All this to state that although one is never wholly guaranteed that the investment will be completely secure in future as things change, suffice it so say investing in this industry is as close as you can get to a guaranteed win.

Amortization:

Ever heard of a debt snowball? With a debt snowball plan, you can apply extra savings to pay off your mortgages faster than initially planned. Say twenty years earlier. In so doing, you reduce the risk involved and increase your income just in time to match that due date of early retirement.

These are predictable ways of determining when and how your wealth grows, and for the most part, you can easily control them. There are various types of real estate investments that help make these ideas practical, and in the next chapter, we get to dive deep into all the best types of real estate you can invest in. Some of these you've probably heard of before or even dabbled in and some might be new, either way, you'll get to know only the best of the best that we know work.

Before we jump into the next chapter, however, let's clarify some misconceptions and myths that have caused a lot of impediment for aspiring or newbie real estate investors.

Myths about real estate investing revealed:

I must admit, some of these myths (okay most of them) really crippled me when I first started out. There were many occasions where I passed on an opportunity because I was still under the false belief of some of these myths and it took me far too long to break free. If only I had known ten years ago what I know today, my real estate journey would have been less nightmarish.

To save you from the pitfalls I kept falling into, here are some myths you need to debunk before becoming a successful real estate investor. Do a self-check as you go through each and see if any of them resonate as that will show you which areas need some work.

Myth #1: Real estate is only for the wealthy.

Actually, it's not just for the wealthy. It's for anyone who is willing to do what the masses won't.

So many people think they need to have money in the bank, high credit scores or connections to succeed in real estate investing. It couldn't be further away from the truth.

The truth is, it doesn't matter how much money you do or don't have right now. It doesn't even matter whether you own credit cards or how bad your credit scores are. You don't need to have any assets whatsoever, to get started in real estate.

Depending on your current situation, you could start as a wholesaler as I did, or you could flip houses. You could also jump in headfirst and start doing rental properties.

As long as you've set your goals right and you have a reliable road map, even without money in the bank, good credit scores or a job, you can still make real estate work.

How?

You must learn the skills needed to be a good salesperson, and marketer. You also need the right skills to speak with investors and get their attention. Leveraging your sweat equity, time and knowledge can be a precious thing when done strategically. The better you get at helping investors see tremendous opportunity in working with you, the quicker you can turn your idea into a profit machine.

One of my real estate friends and mentor told me that when he started two decades ago, he didn't think it would even be possible for him to own 26 units within two years of getting started. That was the impossible goal that he set for himself. It took him eighteen months to crush it and reach his goal. I have countless stories of people who've been able to start from nothing (including myself) and build something meaningful.

Myth busting:

Real estate investing isn't just for the wealthy in society. Anyone can get started in it using different strategies to create income streams that turn the small idea into an empire. The top 1% of the wealthy on the planet all share this commonality. They all participate in real estate investing, and some started with nothing and built great careers and businesses thanks to real estate.

Myth #2: Making money with real estate is quick and easy

This myth is fueled by the "get rich quick" mentality, which never ends well. If you're looking for shortcuts in life and lazy ways to make money where you don't add any value or put in the effort for the rewards desired, then I recommend staying away from real estate.

I know that's not what marketers will tell you. Everyone will attempt to get you to buy into his or her program or product by over exaggerating the truth.

The truth is, like any worthwhile endeavor, real estate investing requires patience, perseverance, and persistence. Believing false stories around real estate riches is setting yourself up for failure. The more knowledge you have, the better you get at execution and implementation, the higher your chances of success in the business.

Myth busting:

Making money in real estate isn't a matter of luck, there are no shortcuts, and it's not a get rich quick scheme. You need to put in the work to reap the rewards. Determination, patience and a success mindset are a must-have. When starting out, you must be willing to invest a considerable portion of your time and effort to produce profit, especially with rental properties.

Myth#3: I need to own my own home before I can be a real estate investor.

No, you don't.

Picture this for a moment. You successfully invest in your first single family home. After which, you rent it out for $3,000 per month. Meanwhile, you're staying in a house that costs you $1,000 per month, and you pay $1,000 as the mortgage for the property you invested in. See where I'm going with this?

Investing in real estate could be an excellent way for you to finance property and have it pay for itself and for your cost of living as well. Simple right?

Myth busting:

You don't need to own a home to become a real state investor. But you do need the right strategy and a little creativity.

Myth #4: I need to form a real estate limited liability company (LLC) first before I can make my first deal.

Actually, unless you are rich and famous and buying large properties of five units and above or commercial real estate, then the simple answer is - this is just a myth. You don't need to form an LLC.

From a practical standpoint, most people starting out have minimal assets to protect. Many people have little to negative net worth.

199

And even if you have a few rental properties, chances are the bank owns 80% of the property, so you don't really own it. No one can take something you don't own. So for the majority of new investors, an LLC should not be a priority.

Myth busting:

You don't need an LLC. I'm not saying you should never get one! What I am saying is that for practical reasons, it can wait until you actually grow a thriving business. Consider the fact that there are expenses associated with maintaining an LLC and most of the time; the perceived protection that an LLC offers can be easily pierced especially if you are an owner-manager. If you have considerable assets then yes, by all means, have legal entities protecting you. If you are a high-profile wealthy person, I also advocate getting one as soon as possible.

But if you're just starting out, trying to hustle to make your first deal happen, you probably don't need an LLC.

Myth #5: I need a lot of experience to be a real estate investor.

It is true that experience makes us better at our craft regardless of industry, but it is not true that you need to have the experience to get started.

Experience is a matter of practice. So if you're just starting out, why would you allow yourself to get hindered by the fact that you don't yet have experience?

Can you remember the first time you rode a bike or drove a car? Did you have experience?

Of course not. It took hands-on practice to learn these skills. The more you did it, the better you became until you attained mastery. The same is true with any type of investing especially real estate.

Myth busting:

It's okay that you have no experience when starting out. That comes over time. Learn as many strategies as you can, implement and experiment to find what works best for you.

Start with basic skills, keep learning and improving. Build upon each skill as you scale to the next level and before you know it, you'll achieve all your goals.

Myth #6: Banks are the only way to finance my real estate deals

This is an easy one for many of us to believe. I totally fell for it too because I didn't think there was any other way for me to get money aside from a job or a bank. But I was wrong...

And I have proved it time and time again that this myth is total BS.

Now, don't be too hard on yourself if you're still stuck in this belief. It just takes a shift in perspective and learning from those who've found other alternatives for financing. In an upcoming chapter, I'm spilling all I've learned so you can be free from this myth as well.

Myth busting:

Although this is usually the common route people take, banks aren't the only way to fund your deals. And if your credit score is as bad as mine used to be when I first got started, no bank will even consider loaning you any money.

Besides, banks cap you out anyways because they have so many restrictive rules and regulations even if your credit scores aren't too bad. Private investors are an excellent alternative and my number one recommendation. All you need to learn is the skill of raising private capital from individuals who are grateful that you can skillfully use their cash and credit in a way that brings them a profit (whatever their idea of profit is). If you can learn to create win-win scenarios and communicate this effectively to private investors, you can quickly and easily grow your real estate business.

Myth #7: Real estate is guaranteed to bring me passive income

Not exactly!

I'm sure you've heard over and over again this idea that real estate investing is a passive investment. There is some truth to it, but you're not being shown the full picture. So let me shed some light here. If you jump in blindly thinking this will immediately become a passive income (and you don't have to lift a finger ever again), you might end up severely depressed when that doesn't pan out.

Certain investing strategies are classified as passive income for the investor, but even these don't just happen magically overnight.

Imagine if you will - investing in a multifamily home where you have long term monthly rent. This is technically speaking a form of passive income, but I can assure you, there's a lot of effort, time, resources and money that goes into the acquiring of this property and the tenants. And although once you have the tenants long-term, you don't need to do very much, as the property investor you'll still need to be involved in maintaining the property.

Myth busting:
Passive income in real estate investing is possible, but even then, the strategy will require some sort of involvement.

Myth #8: I should only invest in real estate that's in my local neighborhood

Many real estate gurus will say that one should just buy property that's within 30minutes driving distance from where they live. This isn't always the best solution for everyone. It indeed wasn't right for me, so you need to figure out what your goals are and then work out a strategy and choose the niche that helps you achieve those goals.

Suppose your goal is to replace your income, retire early and eventually gain full financial freedom but you live in an area where real estate is costly. Unfortunately, your local neighborhood may not be the right place to start because it's highly unlikely that you'll find properties that produce immediate positive cash flow. This concept of just buying where you live is a one size fits all approach, and we all know real estate investing doesn't have a one size fits all solution.

Myth busting:

There is no need for you to feel stuck with your real estate investing if where you live doesn't seem to match the criterion needed to help you reach your objectives. Simply get resourceful and creative, do your research well and find areas that have a low crime rate, where the population is increasing and the price to rent ratio is closer to the 1% rule. In chapter six where we break down the most popular and most profitable real estate strategies, you'll see how to invest in a property that generates passive income while being far away from you.

Understanding the fundamentals

Good real estate investors do not strive to get rich quick. They are not interested in overnight success. Thriving real estate investors enter the game fully informed and aware of the dedication, perseverance, and hard work and self-learning they'll need to take on, and they are willing to go all in.

Are you?

If your answer is absolutely yes - then it's time to step up.

The game is about to begin, and we need to be fully prepped for what is ahead. That means, understanding the basics. There are certain real estate concepts you need to know before jumping head first into the world of real estate investing. Failure to understand these concepts means you will encounter more overwhelm, confusion and roadblocks than is necessary.

Ever been to a doctor's office to get treatment only to come out feeling a bit confused because nothing he said made sense, but you paid a hefty fee anyway and trusted that he knows what he's doing?

It happens to me a lot. Sometimes I come out with a list of medication, take them to the pharmacy and trust that between the words on the paper and the knowledge of the pharmacist, I will receive the right medication prescribed to me which by the way I can't even pronounce. There's a lot of blind faith involved in such situations (for many of us).

Real estate investing should not be like that for you. If you don't speak and understand the "real estate language" you won't go very far. It is your job to self educate and master the language.

Let's start with a basic real estate dictionary to help you out. A more comprehensive glossary can be found at the end of this book.

Basic Beginner's glossary:

1. Appreciation

Appreciation refers to the increase in the value of a property over time. There are many reasons why a property appreciates over time. Sometimes it can be a result of inflation, an increase in demand or a decrease in the supply of properties. It can also be due to added value as a result of property improvements such as adding a pool, upgrading the kitchen or adding an extra room.

Appreciation is usually projected as a percentage of the property's value over the course of a year.

2. Cash Flow

This is the flow of money in and out of business. In the real estate business, it is the rent generated by the monthly rent collected minus all the monthly expenses such as mortgages, taxes, HOA fees, etc. When investing in real estate, always look for positive cash flow from the property.

Gross rent - Expenses = Cash flow

3. Cash Flow Property

This is an investment property that generates a surplus of money each month after all expenses have been paid. Cash flow properties are highly sought after, and they should be your primary target as a real estate investor.

4. Commercial Real Estate

This is defined in contrast to residential real estate and encompasses industrial properties, medical facilities, retail centers, office buildings, and multifamily complexes. Commercial real estate can also be used to refer to land that will be developed into a commercial project in the future.

5. Capitalization Rate (Cap Rate)

This is the rate of return on your investment property based on the income the property is expected to generate. It is used to determine the value of a real estate investment. The Cap rate percentage is found by dividing the net operating income of a real estate asset (expenses minus income) by the current value of the asset. The Cap rate is always calculated using the current value of the asset, rather than the purchased value of the asset.

A simple formula to use is:

Cap Rate = Net Operating Income/Market Value

6. Cash on Cash Return (CoC)

This is the annual return/income an investor receives in relation to the down payment. It refers to the annual cash return of a property divided by the amount of cash invested. If a property is purchased outright with no leverage, this can also be referred to as the property's cap rate. In the case where a property is purchased using leverage, this number differs from the property's overall return, as it does not include the equity gained by the principal portion of the mortgage payment.

A simple formula to use is:

Cash on Cash Return = Net Operating Income/Total Cash Investment

7. Debt Coverage Ratio (DCR)

This is the ratio that expresses the number of times annual net operating income exceeds debt, i.e., total loan payment. A simple formula to use is:

Debt Coverage Ratio = Net Operating income/Debt

•Less than 1.0 - not enough NOI to cover the debt

•Exactly 1.0 - just enough NOI to cover the debt

•Greater than 1.0 - more than enough NOI to cover the debt

8. Equity

This is the difference between the current market value of a property and the amount owed by the owner on a mortgage (if any).

It is essentially how much stake in ownership on a piece of property is worth. If there is mortgage involved then as it gets paid off, the owner's equity grows.

When a property is being sold, the equity is the difference between the purchase price and the sale price. Usually, the market drives the property's equity; however, if a property is improved or upgraded, the equity value can increase.

9. Gross Scheduled Income (GSI)

This is the annual rental income an investment property would generate if all units were rented and the rent was collected in full. In the case where there are vacancies, count that in your calculation at their market rent. A simple formula to use is:

Gross scheduled income = Rental Income + Vacant units

10. Gross Operating Income (GOI)

This is the amount of income needed (that you'll collect) to service the rental property. A simple formula to use is:

Gross operating income = Gross scheduled income - Vacancy and Credit Loss + other income

11. Internal Rate of Return (IRR)

This is the point at which the net value of investment expenses equals the net value of assets income. These are both calculated at the current value of the investment and not the purchased or future value of the property. It helps establish the growth potential of an investment. The IRR can be used to indicate the point at which an investment could become profitable. If an internal rate of return is above a pre-defined number, it is an acceptable investment.

12. Individual Retirement Account Investing (IRA investing)

This refers to using your IRA or retirement account to invest in property. Returns on property purchased with an IRA are generally tax-deferred. However, profits must go back into the IRA account and cannot be spent before retirement. IRA investing allows people to transfer funds to a self-directed IRA to purchase real estate. It's also possible to use it the funds in an IRA account to obtain a mortgage or any other type of investment property.

13. Leverage Return

This is the return calculated on an investment that takes advantage of a mortgage. It should not be confused with cash on cash return. Leverage return includes the principal pay down as part of the return. Although using leverage return is slightly riskier, it is advantageous to the investor as it provides higher yields and enables the investor to diversify across multiple properties.

It is calculated by subtracting the expenses incurred by the property (including the interest payment on the mortgage) from the income produced by the property and dividing that by the initial investment amount. A simple formula to use is:

Leverage Return = Income - Expenses (including interest payment) / Initial Investment amount

14. Leasing Fee

This is a fee paid to the property manager when they sign a lease with a new tenant. If the tenant renews their contract, there is a re-leasing fee.

15. Net Operating Income (NOI)

This is the rental property's income after discounting all expenses. A simple formula to use is:

Net Operating Income = Gross Operating Income - Operating Expenses

16. Operating Expenses

This is the cost of running the investment property. That includes property taxes, insurance, utilities, and all maintenance costs. That does not cover any payments made for mortgages, capital expenditures or income taxes.

17. Operating Expense Ratio (OER)

This is the ratio between the total operating expenses to gross operating income, which is always expressed as a percentage. A simple formula to use is:

OER = (Operating Expenses/Gross Operating Income) X 100

18. Retail Investor

A retail investor is also known as an individual investor or a small investor. These types of investors buy and sell investment asses for their personal account building their own portfolios. They are defined as such in contrast to institutional investors. As a general rule, small investors invest lower amounts than institutional investors.

19. Real Estate Owned (REO)

This refers to a property that is owned by a lender, usually a bank. Lenders generally only take the title of properties after an unsuccessful selling attempt at a foreclosure auction. REO properties are often excellent for purchasing below market value, which makes them highly sought after by investors.

20. Remote Investing

This type of investing refers to the ability to be able to invest in and own property that is geographically removed from your primary residence. In traditional real estate, the prevailing trend was for real estate investors to purchase property that is "in their backyard." This was chiefly because it made it easier to manage and monitor the investment. It often meant the investor would also be the landlord and needed to keep up with daily maintenance and running of the property.

Remote investors, however, do not follow this old trend. They purchase property in areas that have favorable returns. Remote investing allows investors to take advantage of lower property costs or higher rents that may not be available near their primary residence.

21. Rehabilitation

This refers to the repairs that need to be done to make an asset tenant-ready. Primary inspection is imperative before making any purchase to ensure extensive renovations aren't necessary. Rehabilitation can include minor fixes such as paint and lighting upgrades, but they can also extend to substantial repairs such as roof replacement and plumbing upgrades.

In the event of a large-scale rehabilitation, the investor should be notified before the purchase. Costs associated with improvement are generally included in the purchase price.

22. 1% Rule

This is the rent to expense ratio that an investment property must have to be profitable. There are many variables and expenses to take into account but in general, for an investment property to have a positive ROI the rent on that property must be at least 1% of the purchase price. This is considered a favorable investment asset in the real estate world.

23. Single Family Rentals (SFRs)

This refers to a freestanding residential property designed to house one family. It is purchased by an investor and rented to a tenant. SFRs are defined as such in contrast to multi-family property, though properties up to a fourplex are sometimes classified as SFRs as well. Properties with more than four units are called multi-family properties. Families are generally very interested in single-family properties. From an investment perspective, we may consider them steadier as families (especially with children) tend to stay in one place longer.

24. Self Directed IRA (SDIRA)

A self-directed individual retirement account is a type of account that provides tax benefits to money deposited for retirement. Any income from the account is taxed at the tax bracket the account holder reaches upon retirement, which is often much lower than their pre-retirement tax bracket. There is a significant difference between a regular IRA account and a self-directed IRA (SDIRA) account in that the permitted investments aren't identical.

In addition to traditional stocks and bonds, a SDIRA account can be used to invest in alternative investments such as tax liens, notes, and real estate. The money in the SDIRA account can be invested just as the funds in any standard account as long as the dividends are returned to the account. Funds cannot be accessed until the account holder reaches retirement, however. And all asset expenses must be paid for using funds from the account.

A SDIRA can also be used to hold a mortgage although this loan (non-recourse loan), different from regular mortgages is often at a higher rate. It does, however, allow investors to leverage their funds to create a higher ROI.

25. Turn Key Property (TKP)

A TKP is a property that has been purchased, rehabbed and rented to a tenant and is now back in the market for sale to another investor. These types of properties usually provide cash flow from the moment the investor purchases it since the property is already rented.

26. Vacancy Provision

This refers to the money that investors set aside to prepare for a future vacancy. It is a percentage of the monthly rent. The average vacancy provision is 6% for vacancy and 6% for maintenance

You will find a more in-depth list of all the real estate investing terms in the last chapter of this book. For now, you're well equipped to move to the next level of this journey where we discuss the different types of real estate and which ones will be best for you.

Before wrapping up this chapter, there's one more thing I need to mention.

The one size fits all model doesn't work.

It's a broken concept and if you find anyone attempting to teach to you, turn and run really fast.

You are a unique individual with unique skills, goals, motives, and aptitudes. The right model that works to earn me millions may not be the best one to lead you to your millions. We can exchange ideas and insights, and I can even share with you how I search for, evaluate, negotiate and sell my deals for a profit (which I will in this book), but that does not guarantee you will have the same success copying me. It is therefore imperative you become your own influencer.

You must become your chief guru and learn to trust in your gut, your skills, and your ability to make this work. The real estate investment is meant to be the vehicle; you are the driver and the determining factor. If your head is in the game and you've customized your blueprint for real estate success, whichever model you choose will work. Having that right mindset, confidence and trust in yourself are priceless and perhaps the secret ingredient that will take you that extra mile. If you're ready to go all the way, I'm here to guide you into the next phase of this beginners crash course.

Chapter 03: What Are The Risks Involved In Real Estate?

Like any other form of investment, real estate carries with it significant risks. I don't think the risks are higher than investments such as stock market trading and crypto technologies. But since you don't want to go into the real estate investing business blindly, let's make sure you understand the risks at hand. After all, everyone would be a successful millionaire if real estate investing had zero risks involved.

One of the most significant risks in real estate investing is landing on a deal or many deals that turn into negative cash flows. If you find yourself at the end of a deal with less money than you started with, you'll be stuck in what's known as negative cash flow. The issue with a negative cash flow is you'll quickly go broke.

Cash is king in real estate. And you need positive cash flow.

If you don't get good at generating cash flow with your deals, it's going to be tough reaching your financial goals or retiring early. Make sure you learn how to find and analyze real estate investments so you can spot the good from the bad ones. And trust me, there will be plenty of bad deals that look "okay" on the surface.

There's also an environmental risk to take to account. Imagine buying or building a property in an area that was under jurisdiction. Surely that would spell doom for your return on investment. I witnessed such a scenario with an acquaintance some years back. The raw land he bought and constructed apartment complexes hadn't been well vetted. Turns out it was under government jurisdiction, and they ended up in a very long and draining dispute. Do your due diligence well and be smart with the choices you make especially at the start where every penny counts.

Speaking about money, let's talk about the risk involved in getting too much debt for investing. Do you know debt magnifies the investment risk?

The more debt you have, the riskier that investment. And since interest rates are never constant, you can struggle a lot with increased or fluctuating financial costs, which is undoubtedly not good for you. Minimize this type of risk as much as possible.

Another potential risk that could lead to loss is getting stuck with a deal that has no profitable exit strategy. If a deal goes south, and you've already invested in it, how quickly can you exit that deal and will it still profit you?

You must always have a logical, doable, clear and specific exit strategy before getting into a deal. There has to be a contingency plan in place to pull you out of the weeds in case you need it. Whether you intend to do a fix and flip right away or to lease and hold it for 10 years, always have a good exit strategy to mitigate the risk.

There will always be risk involved, but with continued education, proper planning, and some experience you'll be able to do effective risk management as your business grows.

Before going after your first deal, get this right:

The only way to financial freedom, early retirement, and steady passive income is by changing your mindset. Without the right mindset, it doesn't matter how many books you read or which guru you learn from. All of it will be in vain.

Whatever is taking place between your ears determines how successful you become in real estate and in life. You need an abundance mindset, and you need to be right mentally if you want to be a thriving real estate investor. Here's what I mean by this.

On the one hand, you need to have an abundance mindset that recognizes opportunity and trusts in the fact that there will always be someone ready and motivated to sell his or her property. Someone with a problem to which you can provide a solution quickly, effectively and professionally.

On the other hand, being right mentally means you can't just approach this business haphazardly. Whether you're doing it full-time or as a side hustle, you still need to give it the deserved attention and serve your clients diligently and with excellence. You need to be committed, not just interested in succeeding.

Having interest is not the same as being committed. For example, a woman who desires to shed some weight may buy a workout program out of interest. She might even start doing runs around the park once or twice a week because she's interested in getting back in shape. If it rains on that particular day when she ought to be out running, she'll probably skip it and wait till the weather is better. If she has a long week at work, she'll probably skip her DVD workout program for that week and chose to focus on work instead. That's having an interest in training.

Another woman, however, is a professional marathon runner. Whether it rains or shines, she's going to be doing her workout relentlessly. If running in the park is part of her daily routine, she's going to be out there even in the snow. That's being committed to training.

Going to seminars, watching real estate investors on YouTube, reading books and magazines is great and highly entertaining. It can also be very motivating especially if you're being entertained by a high power presenter. But this won't get you results. It will satisfy your interest but not your bank account. Even reading this book can pass as a form of entertainment. So you need to do a gut check because if satisfying your interest is more dominant than the commitment of taking consistent action on the things you learn, real estate will not make you a millionaire. Having an abundance mindset and being mentally committed and in the game of winning is critical. Ultimately, only you know where you currently stand and the results you'll have at the end of this year will be a perfect reflection of that.

How to deal with bad credit scores

Can you really become a real estate investor if you have a bad credit score and too much debt?

There's no simple answer to this. Why?

Because in truth, you can still become a real estate investor. However, it may not be a good idea to start investing just yet. Here's why.

Have you ever taken the time to think about what the credit score even means?

Your credit score is merely a number that represents your financial ability to manage

your money. And before you come to the
conclusion that I'm just trying to be a jerk,
know that I am sharing this advice with your
and ME.

We could all get better at managing our money.
We could all use more education on debt, taxes
and how to improve credit scores. And even
though you don't actually need credit to invest
in real estate, I think it's important to get real
with yourself and recognize where you have
money habits that aren't serving you.

If you do have money habits that are
detrimental to you, no amount of real estate
investing will help you. That's a problem you
need to resolve first.

For most people, poor credit scores are a result
of reckless spending. Buying things you don't
really need to please people who don't even
care about your well-being. Sometimes it could
be a result of an addiction. Other times it could

be the painful student loans, medical bills, unemployment or other distressing situations where one feels lost for options. Regardless of your reasons for a poor credit score, you must make sure you've resolved the problem at the core.

So tell me, what does your written budget look like? Do you even have a written budget?

When was the last time you read a book on credit repair? When was the last time you used your credit card to buy something because you couldn't afford it otherwise? Food is an exception.

If you answer these questions right here and now truthfully, you'll begin to see the relationship you have with credit and how well you're managing your money.

If you're not good at managing credit, you won't be good at handling what real estate investors call "good debt." And even though there are ways to invest without credit (or with poor credit scores), unless you've cured yourself of the disease of credit drama, you'll keep falling into the pit of despair because real estate will never solve your money drama.

Let's touch on ways you can start improving your credit score.

Start educating yourself on how to repair your credit scores. Even though you don't need it now, as your business grows, you will want that option of being able to get a sweet deal from the bank. Remember Kris from earlier? He now wants to invest in a 60-unit apartment, and one of his options is leveraging the great credit he's built up over time.

One of my students started off with less than 300 and has over time built up his credit score to mid 700. He is currently working on the 60-unit apartment building with Kris. The only way this is possible for him is due to the fact that even as a beginner, he's coming in with great leverage that someone like Kris who has more experience in the game is very interested in.

There are countless resources online that can help you slowly improve your credit card, and if though you can still implement what's on this book without credit or with poor credit scores, I cannot urge you enough to work on making it better. Your future investor self will thank you for the work you put it no when it's time to buy your million dollar property.

Let's talk about debt.

Is debt good for you?

Depends on whether you have good debt or bad debt. Trust me, there is a huge difference. The average hard working person can't tell the difference though. He or she generally uses debt to acquire liabilities instead of assets. This is part of the reason financial freedom is so elusive to the masses. They keep buying things that generally lose value over time, and it soon becomes an addiction, which takes years to get out of.

If you want the debt to work for you, you'll need to increase your financial intelligence. You need to learn how to use debt to grow your worth and how to invest in assets that produce cash flow.

Good debt brings you income. It's debt that is used to acquire an investment such as a property, which brings you income and pays for the debt itself. Bad debt just takes money out of your pocket. Credit card debt is a great example.

Did you know that almost half of the US households have some kind of credit card debt? The average amount of this credit card debt is about $10,000. That's crazy!

But what's more alarming is that because there's a deficiency of right financial education, even the people who somehow manage to get out of bad debt soon find themselves in it.

Unless you start doing something significantly different and increase your financial intelligence, early retirement will pass you by. It's good to know where you stand in relation to debt. Credit card debt is one of the easiest traps to fall into. Applying for a new card takes little and swiping away your card has little immediate consequences, but at the end of the month, things start to get a bit scary once you see those interest rates increasing money owed.

How much bad debt do you currently have?

Do you have a plan to eliminate that debt and start building up good debt that helps you get richer? The sooner you can free yourself from bad debt, the quicker you'll achieve financial freedom.

When it comes to using good debt to generate wealth, you first need to shift your perception of debt. Society has primed us to believe any kind of debt is terrible. This is just not true. Good debt (if you know what you're doing) can be very good for you. Imagine getting a loan to buy a property that you rent out for $3000. If your monthly debt is $1000, you'll have a cash flow investment that pays its own debt and puts money in your pocket to cover all your other expenses.

How to invest with poor credit scores and create good debt

As I said before, the good news is you can still become a successful real estate investor even if you dealing with bad debt and poor credit scores. Here are some suggestions that may work for you. I dive deep into many of them in upcoming chapters when we talk more about financing, but I want you to start seeing that as long as you have the hustle, there will always be a way for you to create success in real estate investing.

•Get a hard money lender

Hard money lenders are usually not interested in your credit scores because they care more about the security in the deal. They want to know that no matter what, they'll make money. Many hard money lenders were once investors, so they know the game, and as long as you've done your job securing a great deal, this can be an excellent way to make your money. Remember though, they usually give you under two years to pay back the loan and charge high-interest rates.

•Private money lenders

These are individuals (some you might even know personally) who want to achieve a good return on their investments. They are typically not real estate investors or professionals, and all they want is to know their money is with someone they can trust and that it will yield a profit.

•Seller financing

If you can be smart enough to get seller financing, it can be a powerful way to grow your real estate business without any outside help. It offers a great win-win scenario for all parties, and most sellers have no interest in your credit scores.

•Partnerships

This is a favorite for many others and me. It's about forging alliances with people who complete you but have the same objective. There's something you have that I lack and vice versa. By partnering up, we fill that void, power things up and create favorable outcomes. Perhaps you have bad credit, but maybe you have something I don't such as time, sales skills, hustle, etc. By bringing something valuable and unique to the table, you make it possible for both of us to achieve our goals simultaneously.

Be sure to vet your partner thoroughly and be careful to choose someone with shared values.

• Wholesaling

For those with poor credit, this is perhaps the most talked about method. Every guru is promoting wholesaling and with good reason. If you know what you're doing, you can run an entire deal without using a single dollar of your own money or ever needing your credit checked. But I must warn you - this is hard. It is a job, and you need to be really patient, committed, and because there are legal implications regarding wholesaling, I recommend getting a license first.

Now let's spend some time dissecting the old world of real estate vs. the new world that makes it easier for anyone to become a real estate investor.

Chapter 04: Traditional Real Estate Investing Vs. Innovative Real Estate Investing

Traditional real estate has been the same for the last 100 years or so with very minimum shifts. People usually buy and sell houses using real estate agents as the gatekeeper. In the United States, about ninety percent of transactions involve an agent while the remaining ten percent do private sales. In the U.K agents take up more than ninety percent of the share.

In the old days, this was probably the only business model to follow if you wanted to be part of the real estate game and much of it still continues to take place offline even with the introduction of technology. However, something is starting to shift. The rise of on-demand technology is causing significant changes that are being experienced by the entire industry.

New models are now launching all over the world and investment in the industry is growing. We are now starting to see the emergence of real estate tech companies and innovative entrepreneurs coming out of the woodworks with disruptive concepts that help empower their clients and get the job done.

We are also seeing more creativity in how transactions are carried out.

Perhaps there was a time when you had to be wealthy and have high credit scores to be a real estate investor. That's why people started believing that as the only viable option of entering this business. But as I proved to you in an earlier chapter, this is definitely not the case today. Your possibilities are now endless, and as long as you have the hustle and a good plan, your chances of success are very high with or without capital funding.

Creating your real estate business plan

Creating your business plan is one of the first steps toward long-term success. As any architect will tell you, constructing a beautiful building that lasts over time is impossible without proper planning. This is you ensuring the foundation is solid before breaking ground.

What a business plan is not:

This isn't meant to be rigid rules that constrict you. It's supposed to be a roadmap or a guide that helps you move in the right direction. It gives you a measurable, logical reference point to keep yourself accountable.

With a clearly defined business, you're supposed to feel more motivated, able to envision the end game and carry out the plan from your current starting point.

Here is what your real estate business plan needs to include:

Goals

What objectives matter to you? What would you like to achieve? If you desire to make $10,000 a month from your real estate business, write it down. If your goal is to own 20 units in the next 2 years, write that down. Goals may change over time, and that's okay. As you hit an objective, you'll set a new one and restructure your business. That's how it should be. I recommend setting short-term goals and long-term goals. Make sure these are goals that fire you up and align with your overall vision of your life.

Mission Statement

We've heard from motivational gurus the importance of knowing your "WHY." It's not hype; you do need to know what's driving you to make real estate investing work for you. And it needs to be something deep and meaningful to you so that when things aren't going according to plan (and it always happens), you'll have an anchor to keep you going.

Your mission statement needs to define your purpose, the purpose of your business and how you're going to benefit your clients.

The strategy

As you're about to find out, there are hundreds of ways for you to make money in real estate. That's a good thing. However, you must be careful not to get sidetracked trying to implement all of them at once. In fact, I share the most relevant ones to you in the hopes that you will take just one of these strategies and master it. You don't need to be a master at everything in real estate to make good money. Think of this is choosing a vehicle. You only need one vehicle to move from point A to point B. Your point B is the selected goal. That is your desired destination. Now you simply need to choose the vehicle you'll travel in and stay focused on the journey till you reach the destination. Writing down the strategy of your choice helps to anchor it in. It also gives you the chance to evaluate how well it aligns with your mission, your goals, your current situation and the empire you're building. I've already alluded to the fact that there are many niches and strategies in real estate investing that work regardless of your financial situation. If you're going to work part time or full time on this, you'll also need to pick the appropriate niche and strategy that has the potential of generating the highest return on your investment. Don't worry if you're still unsure which is best for you, come back and fill out this section after going through the next chapter.

Realize also that you can always expand and take advantage of more strategies as you grow and scale the business.

Timeline

Setting smart goals also included giving them an expiration date. You need to pick the desired time that feels realistic but at the same time stretches you. A 23-year-old girl aspiring to be a real estate investor said to me that her goal was to become a millionaire and move to New York by the time she was 25 years old. She gave herself 2 years to go from a complete newbie with no money in the bank, lots of student loans and no mentorship to being a millionaire investor. While it does sound sweet and ambitious, she's setting herself up for failure.

I want you to avoid making yourself the bad guy in the story of your life. Pick a due date for the goals you've just set and do it intelligently knowing that whatever choice you've made, you'll have to be accountable to yourself when the time comes.

The Market

As a beginner, you need to choose an area that you will dominate and the type of properties you'll look for first. You're a new investor with little or no experience so you need to plan on investing in a property that you can easily access. Your local area is often the best and most comfortable place to start because you know the area, feel comfortable enough to live there as well, and it's easy to drive to the property. Of course, there are some exceptions to this in which case you can invest in other areas, but I do recommend starting locally. Identify the local players, start creating allies, learn as much as you can about the properties and opportunities in your local market and you'll find it's easier to become a local superhero. When people trust you, it's easier to do business with you.

Criteria

The next thing we want to make sure you write down in the business plan is a strict criterion of the deals you'll start working on. What kind of deals do you wish to work with? What criterion should each property posses? You also need to define your loan to value, cash flow requirements (critical), the maximum purchase price, the maximum rehabilitation budget, and the maximum timeline. One of my first mentors taught me years ago that having a strict criterion and adhering to it no matter what would save me a lot of heartaches. And he was right.

If a deal doesn't meet your criteria, walk away. Most people won't because they either haven't created a set of rules for themselves or because they get seduced into a deal blindly. Either way, those people usually end up with heart-wrenching stories of deals gone back. I'm not saying you can't land on a bad deal, but at least by having a clearly defined criterion, you can easily recognize properties that won't end up being a good deal, at least ninety-nine percent of the time.

The Marketing Plan

In today's world where people spend most of the time online, it's never been more critical to craft a marketing plan that serves you both offline and online. You can't just depend on traditional marketing methods. According to a study by Facebook, the average person checks his or her phone thirty times a day. However, adults under 40 do it, even more, increasing their range to 150 times a day. And of course, this number is projected to keep growing among all age groups in the coming years. There is great power in technology, and if you're not coming up with creative ways to show up on your clients' mobile phones, you'll not be able to survive and grow in an on-demand environment. So you need to have a marketing plan that helps you reach buyers and sellers effectively. Start thinking of how you can generate constant leads of motivated sellers. Ways for finding the best deals that are listed. Will you use agents, MLS, direct mail to lists, online searches, paid ads or other means?

The Financing

This is usually a very challenging part for many beginners. Today's market requires you get innovative and resourceful especially if you don't have the cash to start with. Write down how you plan to acquire and fund your deals. Will you be using conventional means? Will you get equity partners, seller financing, lease options, hard money lenders or some other innovative method?

There are simple things you can learn to become more attractive to private money lenders which is good because that ensures you always have a steady flow of financing whenever a deal presents itself. We'll cover this more in the chapter on financing your real estate investing.

Your current finances are also essential to include in the business plan. What resources do you have? Are you starting with zero or some equity and cash? Document this and update it as it changes.

Documenting the steps for closing the deals

Carefully write down the steps you are going to use to turn a property purchase into a profit. Include the income and expenses and prepare for the unexpected as well. Detail some of the exit strategies that you know can work in case the plan doesn't go as expected.

Exit strategies

You always need a backup plan for your original plan, and then you need a back up for the backup. I kid you not. Having multiple exit strategies is essential especially in the beginning because without it, you might end up stuck with a property that has no cash flow and that would be hell! So this part should take up a significant portion of your business plan. How are you going to get out of the deal if you need to? Write down as many back up ideas as you've got.

This is where mentorship becomes super useful. Books, seminars, and courses are great, but having a mentor who can share different tricks and perspectives is priceless. That's the stuff you'll never get in a book because it only happens during that live human interaction. A few exist ideas to get you started are, you could flip the property or sell the note or rent and hold. We'll talk more about this in the chapter on the exit strategies.

Building the vision

This is one of my favorite parts when going through this process. It's where you get to paint a detailed picture of the next 10 years and where you and your empire will be. Start in a new page in your business plan document and vividly describe what your business will look like in an ideal (but practical) way. Allow your imagination to take over and show you what's possible. Detail the purchases, cash flow, appreciation, trades, 1031 exchanges, cash-on-cash return and more. Make sure the goals you set, the mission statement and this vision align. You may not know how to get to the vision and chances are the path will not be straightforward but putting it down with as much clarity as possible is the first step toward making it a reality.

One last thing to remember here is that it doesn't have to be perfect and you shouldn't expect the journey to go exactly as planned on paper. It is good to have this detailed document, but you're bound to hit some obstacles along the way and experience some failure. As long as you remain flexible and focused on the long-term vision you defined for yourself, success will be inevitable.

Many investors who've experienced great failure attribute a considerable portion of it to lack of preparation and proper planning. Now you know how to avoid falling into the same trap.

How to invest with little or no money

I am super passionate about this part right here. Coming up with creative ways to run successful deals that turn a profit with no money to is what changed my life when I started out. I want to give you the nitty gritty on how you can invest in real estate without cash or credit.

If you want to make things happen, you'll need a couple of things.

First, you'll need to find the right deal. I have a whole section devoted to this so you'll find helpful tips on how to do this right if you're feeling overwhelmed. Just know, there is a surplus of deals right where you are and with the right mindset and a lot of research you can find one that sets you on the highway to success.

Second, you need to have the right knowledge because if you're not knowledgeable in real estate, you won't get very far. There is no cheating in this industry, those with more knowledge and people skills always come out as winners no matter what anyone else tells you. For those starting out low on cash, this part becomes even more critical as it can become the one thing that gives you an edge and causes an investor to go all in on you and your deals. Do whatever it takes to acquire the right knowledge and continue to learn as much as you can about this industry.

Third, you need to create a way of funding the deals by bringing in someone who can bring in the money. Because when dealing with real estate investing, it does take money. It always takes money; anyone who tells you different is only revealing their lack of expertise in this industry. But the good news is that it doesn't have to be your money.

The best way I've found to make a lot of money when starting from scratch is to either do a lease option or build a relationship with a partner (with a 50-50 agreement) where they bring in the credit and cash, and you run the deals, bring the knowledge, organize a solid team, etc. By leveraging your skills and ability to get awesome deals in play, any good partner with money who wants to become wealthy as well should be more than happy to form a partnership with you.

Kris Krohn pays a great testament to how brilliant this strategy of forming partnerships can be and in fact, said that he made his first million dollars with less than ten thousand dollars of his own cash.

In our world, with the kind of technology today we have available today, finding the money is actually easier than you think. And although I will be talking more about how to fund and finance your deals, here's a great example to copy and paste right now.

Hrishab Bandopadh decided to forge his path to financial freedom by investing in real estate. The only problem was, he had zero cash to fund it and didn't even own a credit card. What he did have was a lot of knowledge and a knack for finding really hot deals. So when he started doing his research, he used a very cool tactic that most self-made real estate investors know about. He went into Facebook and joined all the relevant groups he could find of people just like him that we're looking to build wealth using real estate. It took him about six months of actual relationship building, but in the end, he was able to connect with a guy who partnered with him on his first deal. The rest, as they say, is history.

Today, he says getting into real estate was one of the best decisions he ever made. And as an immigrant who came to America to live the dream, he feels he's definitely found his path. Hrishab especially likes the lease option and says most of his success can be attributed to this method of rent to own homes. He and his partner get these homes for 300% less than market value from and then sells them for their real price.

Think about how different your life can be a few months from now if you can start working on this today. It doesn't matter how old you are, how much money you have or what job you do, making money investing in real estate can be is no longer just a wish, it can become your reality.

Now, if you feel pumped up and ready to get out there, then it's time to dive deep and figure out the best real estate for you to invest in.

Chapter 05: The Best Type Of Real Estate Niches For You To Invest In

Have you ever walked into an ice-cream parlor on a hot summer afternoon eager to get some ice cream only to feel a bit overwhelmed and confused by the number of choices there are? If you ever walk into an Italian ice-cream parlor, the endless options of homemade ice cream will make it tough to choose which scoop to order. The better option sometimes is just to ask to taste as many of the flavors as possible to discover the best one for you. It saves you having to order too many scoops and keeps you from overindulging and feeling guilty afterward for too much calorie intake.

While this is a trivial example, real estate investing is often times the same. There are so many options you could get into, and it might seem like its a good idea to know everything there is about the industry, but in reality, you don't need to know it all, you need to get good at the one or two niches that feel like a perfect fit. Some people know these things intuitively. Others need to test and experiment before honing down on a niche. There is no right or wrong here but let me remind you, getting your niche will be more profitable for you. Don't try to be a jack-of-all-trades. Remember when we said real estate investing is the vehicle taking you to your desired destination of financial freedom and early retirement? Sticking to one vehicle is wise, and that comes from honing down a niche that feels best for you.

Following is a list that includes the most popular property types that real estate investors deal with. You could get even more granular with each of these types if you wanted to. Keep in mind it is not necessary to master them all. This is just an overview to help you understand the options available for you so you can make an informed decision.

Key point: The sooner you can identify a niche that feels right for you, the easier it becomes to establish yourself as a trusted authority and expert. Narrow down your focus as you go through this list, start networking within this niche and execute on your plan of action.

Single family

Many beginners consider single-family homes as the best first step in real estate investing. They are relatively easy to rent, sell and finance. But just because they are easy to get started on doesn't mean you should blindly jump in. Do your market research well; make sure the deal is a profitable, cash flow favorable deal.

The biggest issue with single-family houses especially in certain markets is the fact that the rents derived from a single-family rental (SFR) may not be ample to provide a positive cash flow. Stay away from any deal if the numbers aren't right. Cash flow is your ticket to building wealth and retiring early. Where there's no positive cash flow, walk away quickly.

Small multifamily

These are usually 2 - 4 units. They are often just as easy as the single-family home when it comes to financing and selling and when bought properly, these can produce a good amount of cash flow. They also have less bidding competition in comparison to single-family homes.

One of the upsides of purchasing a small multifamily home is that you only need one loan and if you are a smart buyer, this can turn into a solid investment as well as your personal residence. As a beginner, I recommend focusing on three types of multifamily properties: the duplex, triplex, and fourplex (four units). These types offer the most upside with the least amount of risk for those just getting started in real estate investing and they are also more affordable.

Small Apartments

Investing in large multifamily properties will boost your income while reducing vacancy rates and is, therefore, a more profitable investment strategy for those who know what they are doing. This will require a reasonable amount of due diligence and hustle in comparison to smaller properties, but the cash flow potential is worth the effort.

These are usually small apartment buildings comprising anything between 5 - 50 units. These types of properties rely on commercial lending standards rather than residential ones, but if you can deal with added responsibility that comes with managing these properties, you will generate a much higher return on investment and cash flow.

It's also worth mentioning that these types of properties usually have less competition because on the one hand they are too small for big professional Real Estate Investment Trust (REITs), and on the other are too large for most amateur real estate investors.

Another unique attribute to these types of properties is they are not being priced based on comparable properties aka "comps." Instead, they are evaluated based on the income they bring in which means there's an excellent opportunity to add value by increasing rent, decreasing expenses and managing the property effectively. One cool tactic to use here would be to get great on-site managers who help you manage and perform maintenance in exchange for decreased or free rental space.

Large Apartments

These types of properties are large complexes often with pools, gym facilities, full-time staff, and high advertising budgets. Such properties can cost millions, so this is probably not going to be the best starting point for any self-made real estate investor with little to no cash, but it's still worth knowing that you can invest in it as you build your portfolio.

This class of property although highly priced can produce stable returns with minimal personal involvement which makes it great as a stream of passive income. Many large apartments are owned by a small group of investors (syndicates) who pool their resources. Therefore the more you become a trusted authority and expert, your ability to network, find the right investors and create or join syndication can move you closer to owning these types of properties.

Mobile homes

Mobile homes can be a good investment for a beginner, and they require little money out of pocket. This could be a home in a mobile home park or on its own land. Many of the strategies used in the other popular types of real estate investing can be applied to mobile homes as well so don't be shy to experiment with this type of investing if it strikes your interest.

Commercial

Unless you have a healthy financial situation, I don't advice investing in commercial real estate. Although they can be quite lucrative, they also carry enormous risks and a heavy responsibility. As a beginner, it's good to learn about commercial real estate especially if that is your ultimate goal but take your time investing in this niche.

The purpose, style, and size of a commercial real estate property will vary greatly, but ultimately all commercial properties are leased to some kind of small business. Some commercial investors will rent the building to small local businesses while others prefer to rent out large spaces to big-box megastores and supermarkets. Either way, these types of investments usually provide good cash flow and excellent ROI. There is a downside however that every investor needs to be aware of. These properties often have a more extended holding period sometimes sitting vacant for many months or even years during which time your cash flow disappears. So before investing in this niche market, do a self-check to make sure your finances can handle it.

Raw Land

This niche is for those who would like to own a piece of earth and turn it into a business. Land, on its own, can be improved and then leased out or rented to generate positive cash flow. You could also subdivide it and sell portions or all of it for profit. Some real estate investors like to purchase raw land with the plan of selling it someday for external developments such as a housing development or construction of a freeway.

Private Notes

This type of investment is about buying and selling paper mortgages. Here's what I mean. Imagine you purchased a home with a loan. In that case, a "note" was created detailing the terms of the contract. Now let's assume you decided to sell your property for one million dollars and you offer to carry the full note (thus allowing the new buyer to avoid using a bank loan), enabling the new buyer to make payments of eight percent per year for thirty years until the full one million dollars is paid off.

If at some point you decide that you no longer want to be involved, you can choose to sell the mortgage to a note buyer. The note buyer will then begin collecting the monthly mortgage payments and keep the note or sell it again in the future.

Tax Liens

This opportunity comes about when a homeowner doesn't pay their taxes. In such a situation, the government (local state or federal) has the power to foreclose the home and then resell the property to investors for the amount owed. Generally, this tends to be an incredibly underpriced value making it an inexpensive purchase, which is great if the actual home is a good deal. So don't just blindly chase after deals like these ones. Do your due diligence, crunch the numbers and make sure the home is cash flow positive before jumping into this kind of investing. Tax lien sales are often very complex transactions and require lots of knowledge, experience, and research.

REITs

A real estate investment trusts (REIT) is an alliance that is formed by a large number of individuals who pool their funds together to create what is known as a REIT. This alliance makes it possible for them to purchase huge real estate investments. I'm talking about large apartment complexes, skyscrapers, shopping malls or even bulk amounts of single-family homes.

The process involves buying shares from a company or corporation that owns the real estate properties and then waiting to receive dividends as income. Keep in mind this income isn't tax exempt so you would need to pay taxes.

If you were to become part of such an alliance, the REIT would distribute profit to you and all the other investors. It is one of the best ways to generate passive income and have a hands-off approach to real estate investing as you build your portfolio. However, you should know the ROI isn't usually as high as being hands-on and managing your own investments fully. If you would like to buy shares in a REIT, simply do it via your stock account.

This list is far from exhausted but what you've learned so far are the most popular niches you can get into immediately as you build your portfolio in this industry. Again, my recommendation is to start with one or two niches and gain mastery on them. Build a credible name for yourself then expand as your income, experience, knowledge, and resources expand.

Now, let's talk strategy so that you can get the most out of your chosen niche.

Chapter 06: The Best Type Of Real Estate Strategies

These are the most common strategies to make money with real estate. I have focused mostly on strategies that any new investor can leverage regardless of their financial situation. Bear in mind that in this section our emphasis will be on profitable strategies that are time tested and proven to work even for people with no prior experience.

House Flipping

Flipping houses has become a very popular practice. Perhaps it has something to do with the numerous cable television shows promoting it. Regardless of why it's becoming so popular, house flipping is a strategy I recommend testing out if it resonates with you.

It involves buying a piece of real estate at a discounted price, adding value by improving it in some way and then selling it for a profit. A similar model to help you envision this is the standard retail model of "buy low, sell high."

Since the single-family home tends to be the easiest to buy in real estate, it's the most popular type of property to use this strategy on. When it comes to house flipping, there's a rule of thumb known as the 70% rule. A seventy percent rule means an experienced house flipper will buy a home for 70% of its current (minus any rehabilitation costs).

For example. A home is worth $250,000 if it was in perfect conditions, but it needs $35,000 worth of rehabilitation work. An experienced house flipper would be able to purchase this home for $175,000 ($250,000 X 70% - $35,000) and seek to sell it for the full

$250,000 once the rehabilitation work is completed.

Please note this is merely a rule of thumb and actual numbers verified and adjusted to ensure a profitable and successful flip.

Avoid this mistake:

Don't make the mistake of assuming this is a passive income strategy. House flipping requires effort and active, hands-on participation as well as speed and efficiency if you want to make money from it. In essence, it is like having a job because you only make money when you flip a house.

Speed is essential when it comes to house flipping. You need to buy, rehabilitate and sell the property as fast as possible to ensure maximum profit and to avoid many months of expensive costs like property taxes, utilities, financing charges, condo fees (where applicable) and any other maintenance bills required to keep the house in good physical or financial standing.

Wholesaling

This is a strategy few people know about, and even fewer teach it well. And when done right it can literally launch you into your first millions with no cash down.

Technically speaking, wholesaling is a process that requires you to run a deal without ever owning the piece of property you're attempting to sell. Sounds confusing right? Let me see if I can simplify it more.

The wholesaling process involves finding really great deals, writing a contract to acquire the deal and selling the contract to another buyer and receiving what we call an assignment fee. This fee typically ranges between $500 - $5,000 and higher depending on the size of the deal. In other words, it's about being a middleman who gets paid for finding great deals.

A wholesaler is really great at marketing and finding incredible deals. As a wholesaler, you can sell your contracts to retail buyers or to other investors such as house flippers who are usually cash buyers. This strategy requires someone with strong people skills and someone who is willing to go the extra mile to build solid relationships and credibility within the real estate community. And because most of the buyers are cash buyers, you'll often get paid within days or weeks. It is most definitely a low entry barrier especially if you don't have money to start investing and you can quickly get the experience and connections (not to mention make some real money). Many real estate gurus enjoy promoting this strategy. But do not be fooled, this isn't a magic bullet. You still need to put in the effort and have the right knowledge. And you need to be good at winning people's trust.

Avoid this mistake:

Don't approach this with the "lazy man's mindset." It's not just about finding buyers, it's also about being really good at spotting great deals and motivated sellers who are willing to trust you. Your marketing won't just take care of itself, you've got to be super proactive, and even though anyone can do wholesaling, those who are well equipped with strong marketing funnels are the ones who grow and scale their businesses faster.

If you chose to go with this strategy, be persistent, increase your people skills and wholesaling knowledge, and you will generate a good income stream while you continue to master other more profitable forms of investing.

House hacking

House hacking is a strategy many newbie investors are leveraging when they first enter the real estate arena. It involves purchasing a two, three or four unit property then living in one unit and renting out the others.

Most people will start off with a single-family house when they invest in real estate but smart investors who understand the importance of cash flow follow a different route.

By investing in at least a duplex, you minimize the possibility of becoming a slave to your house expenses such as mortgage, taxes repair and maintenance costs.

The benefit of doing a house hacking strategy is that when done right you could actually live for free. Your property will produce cash flow for you as it continues to appreciate over time.

For example. You could buy a quadplex, live in one of the units and rent out the rest. Since it's still considered a residential unit, you only need to get one loan to cover it, and if you crunch your numbers right and find the right deal, you can end up with a property that pays for all your expenses.

Avoid this mistake:

Don't jump into a deal too soon. Take your time and do as much research as possible to find the ideal one for you that produces enough cash flow to cover your costs. You also need to make sure you vet the tenants thoroughly and implement policies and procedures that protect you and your family in case something goes wrong with the tenants. Most novice real estate investors forget to take these precautionary steps, and it ends up costing them a lot financially and legally.

Live-In-House Flips

This strategy works best for an investor who is very patient, doesn't mind living in a construction zone and also enjoys DIY projects. It is a very hands-on type of real estate investing, but some have enjoyed enormous profits doing it.

Live in house flipping involves purchasing a home that requires a lot of rehabilitation, fixing it while living in it full time and then selling it for a profit.

One of the main benefits of doing this is that when done right, there are no income taxes imposed. Live-in house flipping exempts owners from paying capital gains taxes on the sale up to $250,000 for an individual and $ 500,000 for a couple as long as they've lived at the property for at least two of the previous five years.

Avoid this mistake:

Don't get into live-in-house flips if you don't understand construction and contractors. Too many people are blindsided by issues like termites or cracks in the foundation, which can only be overcome when one has sufficient knowledge and understanding of how construction works. You also need to have an eye for good property deals so that you can get one that will sell well when the time comes.

Lastly, don't jump into this strategy unless you have a reasonable budget in place, cash reserves and a lot of patience. Sometimes the construction work needed may take longer than expected, or the house may not sell when you want it to sell, and you need to be okay with keeping money tied up until then.

Student rentals

Using this strategy won't be glamorous, but it can be very lucrative. Student rental investing is about providing students a great place to live when they leave home and making a significant income in the process. They often give a robust cash flow. You could buy a house for $300,000 and generate $3,500 per month in rental income because in many cases you could have even seven students living in a house paying $500 per room.

One of the major challenges to this otherwise lucrative strategy is the lease. You need to make sure you keep a single contract in place so that the student house doesn't become a rooming house. Which means although there are many rents to be collected each month, they need to be carried under a single lease and with technology, there are lots of simple processes in place to help with this, but you still need to be hands-on for this strategy to work.

Avoid this mistake:

Don't get lured in by the cash flow this strategy generates. Make sure you understand all the financing and legislation aspects required to make this strategy a success. Each city usually has different legislation detailing how it zones these types of dwelling. Some will regulate the number of students per house and also have rules on maintenance, fire safety standards, insurance, parking, noise, etc.

Some cities license student housing at around $500 for the first year and then it drops slightly for subsequent years. There's no denying, this strategy is time-consuming and needs a hands-on approach because most of the students will keep calling for assistance so do your due diligence and become aware of all your costs and responsibilities before jumping in.

Buy and Hold

I consider this to be one of the purest forms of real estate investing. It involves purchasing a property, renting it out for an extended period and eventually selling it for profit. If you invest in a buy and hold strategy, the primary objective would be to rent out the purchased property to collect a monthly cash flow and then eventually selling it out in future profitably.

One of the benefits of using this strategy (if you're doing it right) is that the mortgage on the property will pay itself out through the monthly cash flow generated decreasing your principal balance and increasing your equity over time.

Avoid this mistake:

Don't buy deals that don't yield a positive cash flow. Learn to evaluate properties thoroughly and avoid making the same mistake made by many new investors make. Every decision you make including managing your expenses, choosing the right tenant, managing your assets are all crucial to your success. If done poorly they can result in significant loses. But these are all mistakes that can be avoided with the right knowledge.

There is also a real estate marketing cycle that you need to understand and leverage when making your buy-and-hold decisions.

Every market will be different. You need to identify the ebbs and flow of the marketplace where your property is located. Then you need to increase your education, learn to evaluate properties, find good deals and great tenants.

Short Term Rentals

Short-term rentals are very alluring. They are actually considered the fast way of making money in real estate. This is the Airbnb style of real estate investing where you purchase a property and rent it out on a short-term basis. Usually, the rents are very high, and if your property is in a touristic location, you could charge higher rents and expect to be booked out for most of the year.

Because you're here as a beginner in real estate investing, it's important to remind you that location is everything if you're going to go for this strategy.

The main reason Airbnb properties do so well is they serve as a substitute for hotels and motels. There is also a lot of direct contact between the host/owner and the tenants. Offering a unique and unforgettable experience to your guests is what will help you grow a thriving business with short term rentals so you'll need to either prepare yourself to be more hands-on or hire some professional help.

One more thing you also need to keep in mind is the increased competition from other landlords doing the same, as well as the high turnover of renters who only occupy the place for short durations.

Avoid this mistake:

Get clarity on the type of real estate investor you want to be. If long term, consistent passive income is what you're after, and you want optimal results then don't get into short-term rentals expecting such results. This strategy is not for everyone, and usually, the more dynamic investor looking for short-term gain in real estate is the type who will enjoy this strategy. Get educated on what makes Airbnb properties successful and make sure you're willing to go all in and deliver in both tangible and intangible ways to the clientele that need short term rentals.

Turnkey Investing

This investment strategy has a longer learning curve and can be scary for some, but if you acquire the right knowledge, the benefits of turnkey investing are fantastic. When you hear real estate gurus talking about passive income and getting real estate to work for you, this is one of those strategies that can help you accomplish all that and more. Passive income is the primary objective of investing in a turnkey property.

This strategy is actually straightforward and can be quite flexible, but the ultimate concept behind turnkey is that you as an investor don't need to be hands-on with the investment. Your role is to "turn the key" on a piece of property and make good money from it.

Some investors consider turnkey investing as a property that is already fixed and rented with a third party company managing it. In such as a case all that the investor does is make the investment and get paid any profit.

Other investors consider turnkey investing to be a property that might need some rehabilitation. In such a case the investor would need to fix it up a bit, maybe even find tenants to rent but then turn the management over to someone else. At that point, the investor would sit on the sidelines collecting income from the investment without having to deal with the day-to-day operations.

You get to define what "turnkey investing" will mean for you. Regardless of how you define it, there are two components to always bear in mind.

1. A turnkey investment property is usually not a local property. Turnkey means the amount of effort you put into the investment is minimal especially once the property is rent ready.

2. Your opportunities for investing are unlimited because you can buy the property anywhere.

A major benefit of not being limited to local real estate investing is that you can access areas where houses are for sale for less money. You will be able to buy a property for less, make the property better and then get income from it. And the best part is this strategy allows you to step away from all the work required to own and manage a property (which is usually a full-time job), and just make money. If you do your research well and partner up with the right turnkey real estate company, they might even buy the house first, clean it up and then sell it to you. They make their money by managing it, and you own the property.

Avoid this mistake:

Try not to buy a property without seeing it or knowing its real potential. Understandably, the fact that the property could be a long distance away from you might make it hard for you to personally vet the property. But I still argue against it. Some real estate investors do this, and it's such a gamble. It could work out well, or it could end up being a lemon that costs more money than it makes.

There are always risks involved with any real estate investing but blindly jumping into a deal merely because it's a turnkey investment opportunity is a grievous mistake that's unnecessary. Smart real estate investors do everything possible to gain as much first-hand knowledge of the property before making an investment. I recommend you always do the same even with this strategy.

All the strategies we've shared work. The one best suited for you depends entirely on your objectives, personality and your "WHY." The business plan we created in an earlier chapter will guide you into choosing the right strategy because you'll see which one aligns perfectly with that road map that you created for yourself. This is a decision you need to make for yourself based on how much effort you want to put into growing your real estate business. Now that you're well on your way to your first deal let's get into the mathematics and financing so we can ensure this activity leads you to financial freedom.

Chapter 07: Financing Your Investments

Are you eager to start growing your real estate business but fear it can't happen because you're low on cash?

Let's face it, not everyone is as fortunate as Donald Trump to have a wealthy, well-connected dad who makes the launching of a successful real estate career easy.

Most of us have to start with the little crumbs we can gather, and it's a slow boat to China. But the good news is, despite the limited resources anyone (and I mean you) can get started in real estate investing.

While you can become a real estate investor with no money down, the truth is, money is always involved in a real estate transaction. So one way or another, you have to figure out how to come up with money that isn't yours to make your first deal happen. If it's not your own money, then it will be other people's money. There's a skill required to make you good at getting people to buy into your ideas and give you their money. The more you develop that skill, the faster your real estate business will take off.

Know your numbers

Regardless of what infomercials and hyped up online marketers lead you to believe, there's no such thing as free real estate. It's worth reiterating that over and over again to avoid entering the game with the wrong mindset. Real estate is a commodity, and it must be paid for.

And if you want to get the most out of any deal and leverage the best tool for financing, you first need to know your numbers. Without knowing the math behind your deals, you're flying blind. You must be on top of your debt, you need to know your margins, and you need to calculate operating expenses and determine your return even before making that first purchase. So how well do you know the real estate numbers?

I gave you the basic terminology that you must know in chapter two, and at the end of this book you'll find a more comprehensive glossary to equip you with real estate language know-how, but you still need to educate yourself on the necessary mathematics.

Here are thirteen real estate investing numbers you need to know.

1. Your Mortgage Payment:

For a standard owner-occupied home, lenders typically prefer a total debt-to-income ratio of 36%, but some will go to 45% depending on other qualifying factors such as cash reserves or your credit score. This ratio compares your total gross monthly income with your monthly debt payment obligations.

For housing payment, lenders prefer a gross income-to-total housing payment of 28 to 33%, depending on other factors. For an investment property aim for a maximum debt-to-income ratio of 45%

2. Down Payment Requirements

Owner-occupied properties can be financed with a mortgage and as little as 3.5% down for an FHA loan (see glossary for definition).

Investor mortgages however vary and typically require a down payment of 20 to 25% or sometimes as much as 40%. None of the down payment or closing costs for an investment property should come from gift funds.

Individual lenders will determine how much you need to put down to qualify for a loan depending on your debt-to-income ratios, credit score, the property price, and potential rent.

3. Price to Income Ratio

This ratio compares the median household price in an area to the median household income. Before the housing bubble burst, the price-to-income ratio in the U.S was 2.75. By the end of 2010, the ratio was 1.71.

4. Rental Income to Qualify

Most new investors assume that since the tenant's rent payment will cover the mortgage, they don't need extra income to qualify for the home loan. However, this isn't accurate. For the rent to qualify as income, you must have a two-year history of managing investment properties. You also need to purchase rent loss insurance coverage for at least six months of gross monthly rent, and any negative rental income from any rental property must be considered as debt in the debt-to-income ratio.

5. Price to Rent Ratio

This is a calculation that compares median home prices and median rents in a particular market. To do this, divide the median house price by the median annual rent to generate a ratio.

At the peak of the U.S market in 2006, the ratio for the U.S was 18.46. The ratio dropped to 11.34 by the end of 2010. The long-term average between 1989-2003 was 9.56.

As a general rule of thumb, consumers usually buy when the ratio is under 15 and rent when it's above 20. Markets with a high price/rent ratio typically aren't considered great investment opportunities.

6. Gross Rental Yield

The gross rental yield for a property can be found by dividing the annual rent collected by the total property cost, then multiplying that number by 100 to get the percentage. The total property cost includes the purchase price, all closing costs, and rehabilitation costs.

(Annual rent collected/total property cost) * 100

7. Capitalization Rate

This number is probably even more valuable than the gross rental yield. Mostly referred to as the cap rate or net rental yield, this figure includes all operating expenses for the property. You can calculate this by taking your annual rent, subtracting your annual expenses, then dividing that number by the total property cost and lastly, multiplying the resulting number by 100 for the percentage.

[(Annual rent - annual expenses)/total property costs] * 100

Included in the total rental property expenses are repair costs, landlord insurance, taxes, vacancy costs, and agent fees.

8. Calculating Operating expenses:

Operating expenses on your new property will be between 35% and 80% of your gross operating income (see glossary for definition).

For example, if on your first deal you charge $1,500 for rent and your expenses are $600 per month, you're at 40%

You may also use the 50% rule. If your rent charge is $3,000 per month, expect to pay $1500 in total expenses.

9. Calculating your margins:

As an individual investor, I recommend setting a goal of 10%. Estimate costs at 1% of the property value annually. And don't forget to include things such as insurance, property taxes, monthly expenses such as pest control and landscaping. There's also the landlord insurance where applicable and homeowners association fees.

10. Cash flow

To set yourself on the path of riches as a landlord you need to be able to cover the mortgage principal, interest, taxes, and insurance with the monthly rent. You also need to have cash reserves at hand ready to cover that payment in case you have a vacancy or need to cover unexpected maintenance costs.

Avoid negative cash flow. This usually occurs if you borrow too much to buy the property.

11. After Repair Value

This is simply the value of your property subject to any proposed repairs. Rehabilitating a property inherently increases its value. To calculate how much your proposed renovations may increase your home's value you must dive into some research. Find comparable homes that have recently sold and were in a condition similar to your property's condition and the rehab is done.

12. Repair Budget

For an investment to be successful, you must make and stick to your rehabilitation budget. The budget should reflect all necessary repairs to make your home's condition comparable to those properties in which you used to determine your after repair value (ARV). You need to move fast, create a cheat-sheet for your rehab cost and use round estimates for large items like kitchens, bathrooms, paint, and flooring.

13. Purchase Price

This is also called an offer price. It's essential to making a sound investment because if the offering is too low, you might get outbid and if your offer is too high, you might kill your profit margins.

I recommend you reverse engineer this process. Start by determining your desired return and then subtracting that return and any associated costs from the after repair value (ARV). The resulting figure should essentially reflect your initial offer price.

Now that you've made all these calculation, you're in a better position to make an informed decision about whether a particular property will be a valuable investment so let's move on to how you actually finance the deal.

How to finance your deals

Here are a variety of options for you to finance your first deal as you grow your real estate business.

1. Funding from friends and family

Do you know what Warren Buffet and World Trade Center developer Larry Silverstein have in common?

They both became billionaires after financing their first deals through family and friends. Yes, you read it right. They started small, with the resources available to them and the best part about their strategy is that anyone can do it.

Silverstein actually shared some of his story in a recent interview where he said they were not doing well financially. Silverstein and his father were brokers, which made them very little money. He got tired of living off scraps and told his father they needed to find a way out and become owners; otherwise, they would end up starving to death. Having realized that owners are the ones who make money in real estate, Silverstein and his father made their first acquisition of a distressed Manhattan property by pooling money from 20 people. The Silverstein closed the deal on the building, cleaned it up, refinanced it and paid investors back (plus profit), setting the foundation of what would become one of the biggest real estate fortunes today.

You don't need any startup capital, credit or any of the other criterions everyone else wants. You just need to be good at getting your friends and family to have faith in you.

And in the U.S it's even easier than you think to get friends and family to help you finance your first deal. Get 10 family members to go to FHA (you'll learn what this is below), and have them pool less than $1000, which will allow you to pick up a multifamily property. From there, apply one of the strategies we shared, and you'll be on your way to building your real estate fortune.

2. Trust Deed Investing

This isn't too far from the first tip of family and friends because it's also built on trust. By using this method, you're essentially taking a mortgage from one or more private lenders who would function as a bank, giving them a deed of trust as collateral on the property.

In other words, you commit to meeting the lending terms given to you and if you don't, the private lender (like a regular bank) has the right to foreclose the property should you not meet the terms agreed upon.

More and more real estate investors are choosing this approach offering 8% - 10% APR to lenders to invest in deals with high profit.

3. Federal Housing Administration (FHA) Loans

In the United States, there is a government program that insures mortgages for banks. If you have health or car insurance you probably already understand this concept. It's about pooling money to spread the risk for everyone. The Federal Housing Administrative loan can be a sound way to go about making your first deal happen because, with a small down payment of 3.5%, you could quickly pick up a multifamily property, live in one of the units and rent out the other units producing cash flow while the property appreciates over time.

FHA loans are designed only for homeowners who are going to live in the property so you cannot use an FHA-backed loan to buy a property purely as an investment. Which is why I've suggested getting a multifamily property.

One of the main benefits of financing your first deal this way is that you get to make a little down payment. It's a quick way to get started. However, the downside to this method is that an FHA loan requires additional payments to be made known as Private Mortgage Insurance (PMI). This is a type of insurance that protects the lender and is needed whenever a down payment is less than 20%.

Having a PMI makes your monthly payment slightly higher thus reducing your positive cash flow, but with the juicy income you'll get while holding the property, you could efficiently manage to cover all payments and expenses basically living rent-free while the property pays for itself. Just be sure to find a great deal that produces positive cash flow.

Logan Allec from California shared his success story and how he got started on his first deal in his 20s by using an FHA loan. His first property was a fourplex in a suburb of Los Angeles. It was financed using an FHA loan whereby he put the 3.5% down payment on a purchase price of $435,000 with a $15,000 seller credit. Keep in mind when he got started he didn't have tons of cash in the bank. In fact, he was still paying off student loans but was able to pull this off with just a little hustle and proper education.

He lived in one of the four units and rented out the other three. Since he was young and single, he also rented out the bedroom in his unit and slept on a mattress in the living room. This is what's known as "house hacking," and in chapter six I showed you how to leverage the same strategy if it aligns with your goals. Allec essentially combined a couple of strategies together and ended up living for free, building his equity and generating cash flow for a mere $15,000 out of pocket.

If you're low on cash, whether you're a young millennial or not, this might be the no brainer way to finance your first deal. But let's keep moving on and address other ways you could fund your next deal.

4. Hard Money

This refers to financing that is obtained from a private business or an individual for the purpose of investing in real estate. They usually have higher interest rates, but they give you the flexibility to strike quickly if you have a fantastic deal ready to go. Traditional mortgages are often quite slow and may take around two months or more to close (a very long time if you need to close a deal fast).

I don't consider this a sustainable long-term option for financing your deals, but it is a viable resource when you're starting from scratch with no connections or support, and you come across a killer deal. While the terms and style of this type of financing may vary, there are a few defining characteristics to be aware of:

• This is usually a short-term loan (due in 6 - 36 months).

• The loan is primarily based on the value of the property.

• The interest rates are generally higher (8 - 15%).

• Hard money does not show on your personal credit report.

• Many hard money lenders do not require income verification.

• Many hard money lenders do not require credit references.

• Hard money can often fund a deal in a matter of days making it super fast to close deals.

• Hard moneylenders usually understand when the property needs rehabilitation work.

If you're wondering how to find a hard moneylender, try the following.

Ask a house flipper.

Ask a real estate agent.

Ask a mortgage broker.

Google it.

Use Craigslist.

Remember short-term loans can be tricky. Make sure you understand the implications of using this method to finance it, including all the risks involved with your particular deal.

5. Owner Financing

Banks and other giant lending institutions are not the only entities that can finance your deal. Did you know that?

In some cases, the owner of the property you want to buy can actually fund the purchase. This is the Holy Grail especially for those of us starting out with no funds. If you can do an owner financing, all you need to do is make monthly payments to the seller rather than a bank.

Getting this type of a deal would be like striking gold on the first try. They are usually not easy to come by, but it's not impossible. Often, a property owner will do this for you if they own the home free and clear (they have no existing mortgage on the property) and they want out.

One thing to be cautious about while using this method is to find out whether the owner of the property has an ongoing loan. If the seller does have another loan when selling the home to you, that loan needs to be paid back immediately otherwise you risk bank foreclosure. There's a legal clause written into nearly every loan called the due on sale clause, which gives the former lender the right to call the note immediately due. If the amount can't be paid, then the lender has the right to foreclose on the property. So while owner financing can be a great way to gain ownership of real estate without using a bank, be sure to do some due diligence before signing off on the deal.

6. Buy-2-rent: The Asset-Based Mortgage

Still struggling to come to terms with using hard moneylenders and non-bank agreements? Well, there are other ways to get a deal that is worth mentioning. Asset-based mortgages are one such tool you could use to finance your first deal. Buy 2 rent is a mortgage product from Blackstone-owned B2R Finance and they mainly look at the rental income the property will produce. Unlike traditional banks, this mortgage product doesn't look at personal income (which is great if you don't have a stable income), but they do require a 660 FICO score and other underwriting criteria.

I consider B2R's product an alternative to hard money loans and traditional financing, and since it's based on rental income, it's perfect for real estate investors who are just starting out. By financing your first deal this way, you can get up to 80% LTV for an acquisition or up to 75% for a refinancing. Interest rates range from 6% - 8% giving your start-up a real opportunity to close on properties.

Another great advantage of using B2R is the fact that you have more flexibility and aren't limited on the number of properties you can invest in hence growing your portfolio becomes easier, and you'll never have to deal with traditional financing.

7. Partnerships

Partnerships are a great way to finance a deal, especially when starting out. If you find a really great deal but the price range is beyond your current reach, getting an equity partner might be a better move. You can build a team and bring on an equity partner (someone you trust and bring into a deal to help finance it).

There's no one size fits all when it comes to structuring a partnership. It's something you and your partner will have to agree. You can use the partner's cash to finance the entire property, or they can only fund the down payment. There are no set rules but what you do need is to make a decision on how the deal will be put together, who will make the decisions and how profits will be split at the end.

James Walton, a real estate investor, now closing in on his third year as a full-time real estate investor, says during his first year, after gaining some momentum, he came across an incredible deal that was too good to pass on. He lacked sufficient financing to go at it alone and thankfully, his father in law had been interested in real estate investing. So he became his first business partner agreeing on a 50-50 partnership.

Walton brought the knowledge, experience, and deals and he was in charge of putting the whole thing together. His father in law brought financing and credit. Two years in and now they've done almost a dozen deals together. Not too shabby for a guy who had no experience a few years ago.

If you can find a partner like Walton's father in law, you could quickly build your portfolio within the next twelve months. Depending on your operating agreement, your partner may have an active or passive role, and they may participate in nearly all aspects of the property ownership. An equity partner usually receives a percentage return on their investment that includes cash flow and profit when the property is sold. Unlike private lenders, an equity partnership does not receive an agreed upon interest rate on the loan because they get a percentage of generated income instead. If the property makes a lot of money, then their return will be higher. If the investment loses money, they may have to continue financing to keep the property running until things turn around.

Equity partners take a higher risk than private lenders, but they also have higher returns if the investment is successful.

8. Hybrid Financing: Equity Mixed with Debt

This can come across as complex, but I will do my best to simplify it. Let's assume you have an excellent deal and now you have a gap to fill because you've got 75% of the LTV (check glossary for definition), but you need to come up with the remaining 25% assuming you don't have the cash in hand.

A creative way of handling this problem would be taking out a hybrid loan. Mix the traditional payment schedule of a mortgage with a piece of equity for the lender. But you need to know what you're doing, and you must do your due diligence to ensure you're not dealing with scam lenders and that what you offer them is valuable to them.

The last thing you want is to waste everyone's time by stacking up a hybrid that doesn't make sense to your lenders. Even though private money and mezzanine equity are highly flexible, they also tend to stick to their niches. You have to know what your capital providers specialize in so that you can pick one that will be comfortable if your particular case.

In some deals, you may end up paying a higher rate or give up some control possibly even granting them permission to be active in the investment, but if you do it right and the deal makes sense, you'll end up with a win-win situation.

9. Private Money

Private money lending is similar to hard money in many respects, but it's usually distinguishable due to the relationship between the lender and the borrower. This one is all about relationship building. The better the relationship, the more effective this method will be. In general, the private moneylender will not be a professional like a hard money lender. He or she is usually an individual looking to achieve higher returns on their cash. These types of lenders are generally not business-oriented (at least not like hard money lenders) and the entire agreement is built on a relationship with the borrower.

A private lender will lend you cash to buy the property in exchange for a specific interest rate; however they usually have fewer fees and points, and the term length can be negotiated more easily. This ensures both parties have a win-win situation. When they invest with you, that investment will be secured by a mortgage on the property or promissory note, which means if you don't pay, they can foreclose and take the home just as a bank loan, hard moneylender or other loan types would.

When it comes to interest rate, nothing is fixed. You'll establish that upfront with your private moneylender and the money will be lent for a specific period ranging anywhere from six months to thirty years.

Generally, one investor finances private moneyand he or she gets no equity stake or cash flow or future value outside of the pre-determined interest rate. However, as I said, everything depends on the agreement you make because private capital is extremely flexible.

This is a great approach when you feel confident that you can refinance the property after adding value and I recommend having multiple clearly defined exit strategies to ensure you don't fail to pay the private lender. Just as I cautioned with hard money, private money must be approached with caution, and you need to be sure that the deal is worth the risk.

When it comes to private capital, building relationships and having credibility is imperative. You will need visibility in some way, and you'll have to prove that you are an expert in your chosen niche.

If you want to leverage this approach, make sure you're creating opportunities to highlight your investing experience. Make sure you're growing your online and offline presence. Start a blog, get more active on relevant Facebook groups, attend local real estate investment events, become a member of your local club. The options are endless, especially with today's socially connected world. The more you become a well-known expert; the easier it will be to attract the right private money lender.

Anson Young, a full-time real estate investor from Colorado, is a wholesaler and flipper who is currently working towards becoming a millionaire doing real estate says the funds 100% of his purchase and rehabilitation using private money.

He says, private money lenders typically care more about the deal than they care about your credit score. They want to know you have a solid track record and they want to feel protected by having the first deed of trust on the property, so a hard asset secures their money.

Young finds private moneylenders by either reaching out to his network to find people who want a good return on their money or by reaching out to already established private money lenders who are actively lending in my area. Credibility is everything according to Young. And he's found that chronicling his investment activities through social media is a massive boost as it consistently reminds people that he's in real estate and that he's a professional.

Realize that real estate investing is a relationship based business, and people are investing in you and your ability to execute successfully so anything you can do to build that trust will go a long way.

There are of course other ways for you to finance your deals, but if starting out with little to no cash in hand, I believe these tips will work in your favor and help you exponentially build your portfolio.

Now that you have the strategies and you know your numbers and how to finance them, it's time to talk about where to go to find great deals as well as how to analyze your first deal.

Chapter 08: Finding Incredible Deals

Finding incredible deals has nothing to do with the market and everything to do with the marketing. Most real estate investors who are just starting out fall short of great success because they fail to create a strong enough pipeline of deals. In other words, their marketing sucks. The fact of the matter is, when you have an incredible deal, financing it becomes the least of your worries.

Anyone with half a brain and a desire to make more money will be willing to at least partner with you if you can show them a deal of a lifetime. So although most people think money is the biggest obstacle in building a successful real estate business, I have found the real hurdle is getting a robust pipeline of amazing deals.

345

Every savvy real estate investor needs a process that leads to a successful result. Have you figured out what your process will be?

In this chapter, I want to help you overcome that obstacle as much as possible. To start us off, I want to share a simple system that Biggerpockets.com evangelizes. They even have an entire resource that you can download on their website to help you dive deeper into this system if it resonates with you.

The LAPS Funnel

This funnel represents a process detailing the journey you need to take each time you want to close a profitable deal. Leads - Analysis - Propose - Success is one of the most straightforward processes you can emulate to start closing great deals.

346

Leads:

You need to source channels that offer you consistent, high quality leads. With the rise of technology and social media, I recommend compiling a list that includes both offline and online channels. Your goal at this first phase is to get as many fresh leads as you can into your funnel and then filter them out until you're left with just a few hot deals.

For example, I might gather 1,500 - 2,000 leads and only end up buying one property. The raw leads are the top of the funnel and could be any potential lead coming from direct mail list provider, driving for dollars, FB paid ads, MLS or something else. Once I have the raw lead, I start the qualifying process so they can turn into a hot lead. Hot leads qualify for the next phase.

Analysis:

An accurate analysis of a deal will include the four quadrants. Income, cash flow, expenses, cash on cash return. You not only need to know these terms and what they represent but you also need to run the calculations on each of them before signing off on any deal. For any property, there is a value that will make it worth buying and your job is to discover that magic number through a detailed analysis of the property. You also need to conduct a preliminary title search to make sure the property may be sold.

Analysis requires massive action, lots of research and enough knowledge about the market and this industry as a whole. While I may have started with up to 2,000 fresh leads which narrowed down to 100 hot leads, I might only analyze half of them (50 properties). So if you're not willing to put in the hustle, your efforts will fall short here, making it tough for you to find the right deals that will set up a foundation of success for your business. Do not shortcut this step while going through the process.

One of the key benefits of doing a thorough analysis and knowing your numbers is that you get to avoid falling for bad deals that look good on the surface.

For example, suppose you found a deal that was asking for $250,000 for a duplex. While doing your analysis, you realize it would take $200,000 to rehab the property and would therefore only be worth paying $50,000. Sometimes you might even find a maximum allowable offer is actually a negative number meaning they would have to pay you to take the property off their hands! In such a situation, going through proper analysis helps you avoid the frustration of making an offer on a deal that would become a headache.

Propose:

This phase involves making an offer. Now that you've done a thorough analysis of the properties and you've found something you love (and the numbers make sense) there are a variety of ways you might make an offer. You can do it formally through an agent, in direct conversation with a seller or online through a real estate auction site. Regardless of the channel you use, if you want to buy a deal, you need to make an offer.

Once the offer is made, prepare for the rejection! As with anything else whether it's a job interview, prospecting or even trying to get a date, not everyone will accept the offer given. After all, you are dealing with human beings even in real estate, and they reserve the right to say no. Most of your proposals will probably never get accepted, and that's okay.

You must learn to love rejection and change your mindset around failure. Just because a deal doesn't go through or a proposal doesn't get accepted doesn't mean something is going wrong. Sometimes, it's for your own good. You might find rejection is just another stepping stone to something even greater.

For the offers that do get accepted; you now come one step closer to closing your first deal - our last phase in this funnel.

Success:

This is where you put the deal together, seal it under contract and do your best to ensure everything works well. Remember, in real estate, even if a deal is under contract, there's no guarantee that it's going to result in a closed deal. Although the bottom of your funnel is narrow and its purpose is to close the deal, you still need to be agile, open minded and vigilant because things rarely go according to plan.

In theory, you should be able to close on any deal once it's up and running, but we all know business isn't so black and white.

For example, I recently had to let go of a deal that didn't pan out because the seller withheld some pretty crucial information. I already put out the contract, and everything seemed to be going great, but I soon discovered the seller still had a mortgage on the property. He owed more money to the bank than I was paying him yet hoped the deal would go through without me noticing his bank debt.

So I packed up and moved on to the next offer that I was working on. This is the power of having a funnel that works. Of course, there's more to it than just this funnel but this is the process I have learned, and it seems to be the same process all the best real estate investors use to fill their pipeline with potential deals consistently.

Powerful tactics for finding great deals

Before we move on to the next chapter, I want to share some tactical examples of how you can literally find your next deals and fill up your pipeline fast.

1. Word of Mouth

The old fashion way is sometimes the best way. By letting everyone know that you are in the

real estate business and that you're in the
market to buy, you'll place yourself in the best
position to find great deals. Networking with
peers, joining your local real estate club or
even online forums and marketplaces is a great
start.

2. Newspaper

Although digital technology is taking over and
hardly anyone uses traditional newspapers, the
classified section of your local paper might still
be a great place to start looking for homes that
are for sale by owner.

Real estate agents usually also put their listings
in the newspaper so it can be challenging
figuring out what's also listed on the MLS and
what isn't, but it's still a great starting point.

3. Multiple Listing Service

The Multiple Listing Service (MLS) is a
collection of properties for sale by different

real estate brokers across the country. When you go on sites like redfin.com or realtor.com, you'll be searching on the MLS, and the information found there is available for anyone to take advantage of.

4. Craigslist

Craigslist.org is a free classifieds website and one of the most popular sites in the world (number 51 to be exact). Millions of people are using Craigslist daily to buy, sell, trade or give away nearly anything you can think of under the sun. Real estate is no exception. If you know what you're doing, you could easily find some good potential leads within Craigslist.

5. Bank foreclosed property

You can easily get a great deal on foreclosed properties if you know how to do things right. Generally, these deals come about when a homeowner fails to pay a mortgage payment for an extended period forcing the lender to repossess the property and resell. Of course, it's sad for the homeowner who just lost the property, but once it's done, the property can become a great opportunity for you assuming the rehabilitation isn't too serious. Talk to your local real estate agent about foreclosures in your area and start checking some out. You might be surprised at the deals you can get.

6. Driving for dollars

Simply stated, this tactic involves you getting into your car and driving up and down the streets of neighborhoods you want to invest in, looking for potential deals. Usually, you want to focus on finding properties that seem vacant, distressed or transitioning negatively. For example, a property with 18" high grass is an indication that someone doesn't care about the property that much.

While driving down the neighborhoods you want to invest in, you'll likely encounter dozens of potential properties. Write down their addresses including notes about the condition of the place and take some photos as well. Then once home the real research begins. You might need to do some digging into the public records to find the owner of the property, or you might even do a reverse phone number search to the owner's number.

It's one of the lowest cost methods especially if you're just getting started and you're low on marketing or advertising funds. It also helps you understand the neighborhood better and of course the ultimate goal here is to capture as many raw leads so you can bring them into your funnel and eventually close the right deal.

7. Wholesalers

This is one of the best tactics to use especially if you already know a wholesaler. Wholesalers love putting deals together, and they already know creative ways of finding incredible deals so why not partner up with one?

For example, you can get a wholesaler to find a deal and put it under contract for $120,000 and then have them sell the agreement to you for $125,000, netting a $5,000 profit for himself/herself and enabling you to score a great deal in the process.

But you must find a good, trustworthy wholesaler. Finding a wholesaler isn't always easy but the more you network in your local marketplace and online, the easier it becomes. You could also train your own wholesaler who goes out and finds the deals for you.

8. Direct Mail

This is the act of sending out a large number of targeted letters or postcards to people who might be interested in selling their property, knowing that at least a small percentage might call you to talk more about the possibility and out of that small percentage, few will end up actually selling you their properties.

It's true none of us value direct mail anymore, but it isn't a lost cause. Sure it needs way more creativity and a solid plan backing this tactic, but if done right it can be a great way to generate great deals because most of the time, the people who will agree to sell you their properties are motivated sellers who don't want to deal with real estate agents. Direct marketing makes it easier for you to find an owner with a problem so you can help them solve it. It's not about tricking or taking advantage here, it's about building a reputation for yourself that you not only make money in real estate investing, you also help make a difference in people's lives.

There are many "lists" you can buy and mail to, but the most common is the "absentee list." This means that the person who is on record for owning the property doesn't live at the property. Companies like ListSource.com or MelissaData.com can help you find and purchase lists, and you can send letters, postcards or whatever creative method you prefer. The cost of sending a postcard is around $0.50 each, and a letter is about $1.00 each depending on how much work you do and how much you outsource.

It's important to mention that this tactic requires repetition. You can't just test this out once. Find a way to regularly reach out to the group you desire to connect with and build a rapport of some sort. And you also need to develop a brand and credibility both online and offline because the more your potential leads trust you, the easier it will be to strike a deal.

Chapter09: The Unsexy Stuff No One Likes To Talk About That You Need To Know About Before Your First Deal

Managing a full-time job and real estate.

More and more people with no prior real estate experience are quitting their jobs and going in full time to build their fortunes because as you might have guessed, it's not being viewed as one of the best ways to gain financial freedom. But not everyone should just quit their job. Sometimes, it's not even the right thing to do.

If you were wondering whether it is possible to keep your job and still grow a real estate business, then this chapter is for you. You can absolutely keep working a day job while expanding your portfolio.

In fact, one of the benefits of keeping your job and becoming a real estate investor is that you don't become dependent on it at the start. The cash flow generated by your new investments can go into exponentially growing your portfolio while you live off the salary from your day job. This can quickly fast track your business.

Having a stable income also helps with financing because banks will be more willing to help you out when you've got a credible 9-to-5. So if you already have a day job, don't just quit, there's much good that can come from it and you can already begin growing your portfolio by investing in a buy-and-hold deal with property management, partnering in a larger piece of property, investing in mortgages (notes) or serving as a private money lender.

There really is no right or wrong way to approach real estate as long as you have clarity on how much effort you're willing to put in. Whether you do it full time or part time you can still work your way into financial freedom. The most important thing is that you do a self-check and follow your gut when it comes to starting this. If you're unemployed, the choice is plain and clear, but if you currently have a job, please don't just quit because you hear people on YouTube advertising how they quit their jobs and made millions. You need to follow your own path and make informed decisions if you want this business to succeed.

That said, it's important also to emphasize that you can be able to figure this out on your own regardless of whether you do it full time or part-time. Real estate investing is not rocket science, and there are countless stories of average individuals who have self-taught themselves into vast fortunes.

A common question many new investors will ask is:

Do I need a guru to be rich?

The simple and short answer is absolutely not! You don't need a guru for anything really because you are the determining factor in your life.

Whether it's a health, relationship or financial goal, only you can make it happen. Oftentimes gurus are just external motivators.

However, I do recommend getting some kind of mentor. A mentor does not need to be a guru, and quite frankly I hope you get a mentor that isn't a guru because at least they will genuinely make time for you and help you walk this path of real estate investing without the hyperbole of fancy cars, models and getting rich quick. It is, in fact, true that there's a real estate guru trap you need to avoid, but that doesn't mean you shut out all experts. Some individuals are very knowledgeable and genuine, but you must do your homework and refuse to get caught up in the hype, empty promises, and wishful thinking.

How do you deal with expensive markets when starting out with no money

It's tough to start out in an expensive marketplace if you've got no cash in hand. There's no easy way around this. The best thing you can do is to get creative and innovative. Utilize the resources at hand, amplify your skills and use all the tricks, strategies and options I have detailed in this book. Without persistence, perseverance and lots of creativity, you just won't go very far regardless of the marketplace you're in. I have shared several strategies of how you can start small, how to find private money lenders or partner up with someone who has what you're lacking and you've read numerous stories of people who've been able to succeed even when the cards were stacked against them.

If your market is tough to crack and you really don't have the cash, consider the Turnkey investing option we talked about. But even then, do your due diligence and make sure it's right for you.

Before we move on, there's one more thing worth talking about that most skip over.

Getting an LLC. When should you get it and how do you start?

Many novice real estate investors are usually confused about getting an LLC, so it's only fair we touch on it here. And then you can make an informed decision over when you'll need one.

Not every real estate investor needs an LLC especially those just starting out, but of course, as your business grows it is advisable to get one.

A limited liability company is meant to protect you from potential lawsuits related to the property. Suppose you invest in a property, rent it to a tenant who decides to throw a big party, during which one of the tenant's guest falls over a balcony. If the injured guest pursued a claim based on the "unsafe condition" of the rental property, you would be named in the lawsuit. And you'd be forced to defend your personal assets (all of your personal assets), from the plaintiff's claims. If, however, a Limited Liability Company owned your property, your risk of exposure would be insulated by the protection of the company, leaving only the assets held by the LLC exposed to that lawsuit.

Nevertheless, the trouble of forming and maintaining a company may not be worthwhile protection anyway, especially if you breach some of the clauses (which will often happen for self-starters and small business owners who often co-mingle personal and business funds). There are other affordable options if you're just starting out that could protect you from the theoretical threat of a lawsuit. An example of this getting liability insurance.

Liability insurance is more affordable but beware, it has lots of carve-outs and limitations so take the time to understand exactly what you're getting by using this alternative option.

If you wish to minimize the risk, you just need to improve your chances of success by choosing the right strategy and complying with the corporate formalities required by applicable laws where you live, even if the steps are at times tedious and somewhat confusing.

If you are serious about building a future and a fortune in real estate, you should at least consider whether or not the acquisition through an LLC is the right choice for you. If so, it's better to start an LLC right off the bat as you make your first purchase instead of waiting to transfer the real estate to an entity at a later date where you might need more people involved (like your lender). An LLC doesn't necessarily offer any more or less protection from outside lawsuits than a properly formed and operated corporation or limited liability partnership, but it does provide enough benefits particularly for those just starting out.

To get started on your limited liability company I recommend following these five simple steps:

Step One: Choose Your State

As a new real estate investor, the best option is to form your limited liability company in the state where you live and where you plan to conduct your business. If you plan on investing in properties in different states, then you'll need to register for a foreign LLC in every state where you'll do business. You should know however that although business-friendly states like Nevada are great for registering your LLC, there's a lot of paperwork and extra fees involved.

Step Two: Pick a Name For Your LLC

Every state has its own rules about the kind of names an LLC can have. Do a name search online and learn about the laws in your state and pick a suitable name. Here are a few guidelines to help you get started.

• Your name must include the phrase "limited liability company" or one of its abbreviations (LLC or L.L.C)

• You may be required by some Banks or Attorneys to provide additional paperwork and have a licensed individual (doctor, lawyer, etc.) as part of your LLC.

• Your name cannot include words that could confuse your LLC with a government agency (FBI, Treasury, State Department, etc.).

Step Three: Choose A Registered Agent

The next thing you need is to appoint a registered agent (either a person or a business) that will send and received legal papers on your behalf. Official correspondence documents such as legal summons and registered filings will be received by your registered agent and forwarded to you.

Most states require every LLC to nominate a registered agent. This agent must be a resident of the state you're doing business in, or a corporation authorized to conduct business in that state.

Step Four: File Your LLC With The State

The fourth step you must take is to file your documents with the state. This is essentially how you create an LLC. This document is usually referred to as "Articles of Organization" or "Certificate of Formation" or "Certificate of Organization. Your LLC document is meant to outline the organizational structure of your business. You'll also need to decide between appointing a manager for your LLC or have it be co-managed by the owners.

Step Five: Create An LLC Operating Agreement

The last step before you're ready to make your first purchase under your new LLC is to create an operating agreement. This is a legal document that outlines the ownership structure and member roles of your new LLC.

The good news is that most states in America don't have this as a requirement, but I still encourage you to create it anyways. Check in with your state to find out if it's mandatory. There are six main sections of an operating agreement.

• Organization - describing when and where the company was formed, who the members are and how ownership is structured.

• Voting and Management - addressing how the company is managed as well as how the members vote.

• Capital Contributions - covering which members financially support the LLC, and how more funds will be raised in the future.

• Distributions - Outlining how the company's profits and losses are shared among members.

• Membership Changes - Detailing the process for adding or removing members, as well as when members can transfer their ownership shares (if applicable).

• Dissolution - Explains the circumstances in which the LLC may be dissolved.

After following these steps carefully, you'll now be the owner of your very own LLC. After which you're ready to start growing your real estate business with more ease and peace of mind.

I do recommend also obtaining an Employer Identification Number (EIN) once you've formed the LLC. This is like a social security number for your LLC. And remember, you must separate your personal assets from your business, register your LLC for state taxes, set up accounting, and get yourself more protection with business insurance especially if you're going to be a landlord.

With all this knowledge in place, it's time to give you a simple process to help you go from ideation to your first purchase. As a beginner, if you do these four things diligently, you will close your first deal successfully.

The 4 steps to real estate success

The only secret sauce that will enable you to start winning with real estate from your very first deal.

• Find the deal

The first thing you need to do is find an incredible deal on a property that you love. If you don't love the property, don't invest in it. And the trick here is to find a deal that you love because the property resonates with you and the numbers are also good. You can't afford to compromise on either of this if you want to hit a home run.

How do I find the deal?

Well, I have shared so many tactics and ideas on where to start looking for deals in this book. Check in your local paper, visit trusted websites like Zillow go on MLS sites or call up real estate agents in the area you want to do business. If you are going to flip houses or do wholesaling, paid ads are also a great channel and when leveraged properly social media can bring you lots of leads with just a tiny budget.

Make sure you have your criterion clearly outlined when you start finding your deals.

Read through all the ideas contained in this book several times, test them out, drive for dollars if you have to, build relationships with real estate agents so they can keep you in the loop on hot deals.

Get creative and leverage social media and paid advertising if your budget allows. Whatever you need to do to always have a full pipeline of potential deals - do it!

Real world example:

Let's assume you live in Philadelphia and you've landed on an incredible 4-unit deal. This feels like the right fit for you. You have enough knowledge, and you've decided it's time to take the leap of faith and invest in your first property. The property is a 3,656 sqft that goes for $260,000, and since you're doing it as a private residential purchase, you can expect a down payment of 5%. Now it's time to talk about where you can get the money.

• Financing the deal

Most people think this is the biggest obstacle to closing that first deal, but in truth, it isn't. If you have an incredible deal finding the resources to make it happen won't be impossible. You can go to any American Bank to finance your deal. You can use one of the many alternatives I shared in the chapter on finance, and if you are going to live in one of the units (I highly recommend this strategy when getting started) then you can get an FHA (see glossary) so you can get the best loan with the lowest down payment.

How do I finance the 4-unit property that costs $260,000?

By living in one of the units, you could easily go to FHA and put 5% down which amounts to $13,000. Essentially, you'll be the owner of a property that's worth a quarter of a million dollars, yet you only invested $13,000 and if you can do the next steps right and hold on to this property long enough, in 30 years the property will be debt free, and it will have appreciated in value.

•Analyzing the deal

This is where you get to test and see if the 4-unit property makes sense to invest in. You must do a preliminary title search to ensure the property is good to invest and also to ensure it's worth the investment.

The most important thing when analyzing your first deal is to figure out whether the property is profitable in terms of cash flow. You also need to know if the numbers make sense in relation to cap rate; the internal rate of return and you must work out the cash flow before and after taxes. The mathematics doesn't need to be complicated or overwhelming. Keep it as basic as possible, use the formula outlined in the chapter on financing as well as the formulas I shared within the glossary. There are also many resources online like Biggerpockets.com that offer online calculators to help you analyze deals quickly.

Getting back to our 4-unit property, here are some basic calculations that would apply here.

Property = $260,000

5% down payment = $13,000 which means you need to finance $247,000. The debt that you'll need to pay annually can be rounded off to $15000. Annual income from this will be $34,200. The expense of maintaining this can be assumed to be 50% of your income as a fair approximation, but since you're managing the property and fixing it, the cost should be lower. So let's assume this will cost you $12,000 annually. That leaves you with $22,200 - $15,000 = $7,200 positive cash flow which is about 50% ROI on your original down payment. Not too shabby for your first deal.

This is a fundamental example of how you must analyze your deals.

• Managing the deal

Assuming you're going to fix and maintain this first deal, the cost of repairing and running the place should be kept minimal, so it doesn't eat up on your profits.

How do I manage the deal?

To get the numbers I just shared above using that FHA loan, you need to fix and manage that property yourself. You also need to live in it for the first year. And you must continue paying yourself rent as well if you're a savvy investor. If you do your job right as a property manager, you could comfortably raise the rent on the property. Even as little as $50 per

month annually, you'll be amazed how fast
your income can grow over time. By now I am
sure you can see that you don't need hundreds
of thousands to start your real estate journey.

Chapter 10: Profitable Exit Strategies

Exit strategies are plans that smart real estate investors make to ensure they can exit a deal profitably. The correct approach will result in maximized profits and minimal risks, therefore, take your time making the decision on which strategy to implement.

What most successful real estate investors know that you don't:

Even the best real estate exit strategies can go wrong. They may not work, and you need to be prepared and counteract potential obstacles with multiple approaches.

A backup plan is critical, and you need to always have yours ready. Wondering what might go wrong with your exit strategy?

1. You might have unexpected maintenance costs that cancel out your profits.

2. You could get tenant issues resulting in lost rent.

3. You could struggle with management and end up with poor property management, which can diminish the value and hurt potential cash flow.

4. You might experience a distinct lack of demand, failed escrow or the backing out of a lender, which may hinder the flipping of a property.

5. Depreciation may occur.

And these examples don't even begin to cover the long list of what could go wrong. I say this to make you aware of the fact that you need to be prepared for anything. One exit strategy is never going to be enough. That's why I am sharing several!

Here is a list of exit strategies you should consider until you find what's the right fit for your particular deal.

Prehabbing

This exit strategy is actually a hybrid combining rehabbing and wholesaling. During pre-hab, minimal work is done (as opposed to flipping where lots of rehab work is done), to bring the property up to selling quality. This option is great if you're a DIY type of real estate investor, but you don't want the full commitment required in a fix-and-flip deal. Simple ways you can pre-hab a property includes updating the landscape, replacing the carpet, doing a new paint job on the interior and exterior, etc.

Prehabs are usually not difficult, and they are inexpensive, and they are often limited to improvements that do not require a professional.

Flipping

This is one of the most popular and arguably most profitable real estate exit strategy because it will allow you to sell the target property at full market value. The formula for success when it comes to flipping a deal involved finding a property at under market value in a market where demand is strong, putting together a reliable team of contractors, sticking to the rehabilitation budget and timeline and then finally selling the property quickly to the highest offer possible. Rehab requires you to purchase a house, fix it and then sell it for more than the original investment cost, which includes purchase, and repair costs. There are so many factors to consider when doing a flip so make sure you learn as much as you can about flipping houses and real estate markets beforehand to avoid significant loses.

Wholesaling

When starting out with little to no cash (which is what this book has focused on), this might be one of the best exit strategies to implement. You (the investor) will necessarily act as the middleman between a motivated seller and an end buyer. Your role here will be to find and quickly sell a property for a respectable profit margin.

You have two ways of doing this:

You can sell or "assign" your purchase contract to an end buyer, or you can actually close on the property and immediately resell the property to another investor in what's known as a "double close."

The best part about this strategy is that you don't need to invest any personal cash in facilitating this deal and you'll instead make money via your wholesaling fee. Many new real estate investors prefer this strategy because it really is the easiest way to get started.

Lease Option

This exit strategy is more commonly known as rent-to-own, and it will allow you to rent out the property to a tenant, but with the option to purchase at a later date. Usually, an agreement will be made between you and the tenant for a rental period, after which they can begin the purchase process. Once the rental period ends and the tenant decided to move forward with the purchase, their monthly payments will then be made toward the purchase of the property (similar to mortgage payments). The payments are made directly to you instead of a lender.

Seller Financing

This is an innovative technique that permits the owner to sell the property to a buyer. If you choose to use this as your exit strategy then essentially you would (as the owner) finance the deal and act as the bank. Then you will receive monthly payments. As the seller, you will be required to maintain the mortgage loan to cover the sales price and the reason it works so well is because of the flexibility it provides to both buyer and seller. You wouldn't need a middleman or financial lender and the closing process is swifter. It also helps your listings stand out in the market since you'll be allowing buyers to finance the purchase through you.

It's also worth mentioning that seller financing can also create a good source of monthly income and it spreads out tax requirements as well (if done correctly).

As a buyer using seller finance, one of the key benefits is being able to negotiate to put little to no cash for down payment, and it enables you to buy more properties without affecting your credit report.

Buy and Hold Real Estate

The example I shared in the previous chapter is a perfect example of investing in a property that could have a buy-and-hold exit strategy. Once you have the property and have a positive cash flow, you could choose not to sell it and instead receive the money cash flow for as long as possible. This strategy however always includes some rehab work on the property to increase the value, quality and market price of the asset. You will be able to raise rental rates and build up equity in an asset with this exit strategy. However, it comes with its fair share of headaches and responsibilities as you manage the property.

Bank Owned Homes

A bank owned home or real estate owned (REO) is a property that is being sold by a lending institution such as a bank.

When a foreclosure happens on a property, the financing entity will seize it back into their possession and sell it under market value to a new buyer. Since it's expensive for banks to hold and maintain these properties, it's in their best interest to sell them as soon as possible and to do so they will usually remove any outstanding liens and debts from the property. Bank owned homes are usually sold through real estate auctions or through the lender's special REO listing website.

Please note this isn't a standard exit strategy and certainly not easy to use as a novice real estate investor but with time and experience you can to navigate real estate auctions and leverage this strategy to get some great deals.

As an investor I expect you to delineate between each of these options based on your desired outcome. The strategy you choose will depend on the amount of cash you want to invest and your level of experience. There's no wrong or right way of doing this, but the more educated you are about your options, the easier it will be to navigate the deal and find the most profitable exit strategy.

Chapter11: Growing Your Empire

Once you've successfully executed on your first few deals and you get some momentum going, you can start scaling your real estate business. Start small, grow steadily and scale it exponentially at the right time. Don't try to skip over the learning curve.

Your education and the experience you get starting with a basic 2 - 4 unit property and building toward larger units until you are ready for commercial real estate is priceless. Honor the journey, embrace and enjoy the process. The hustle, dedication, patience, and persistence you put into this will be richly rewarded as you watch your wealth and real estate portfolio grow over the next few years. It doesn't really matter how you start. Whether you have some cash in hand or no money at all, you are now fully equipped to make something happen.

No more excuses.

If you genuinely want financial independence and you want to retire early and focus on things that matter to you then now is the time to take action in that direction. Remember not to compromise on your cash flow especially in the beginning when you're laying the foundation for success. If a property isn't producing at minimum 5% cash flow, keep looking until you find that first deal that will set you up for success. Before evaluating future projections, value adds, location and so on make sure the numbers are right and that you get positive cash flow out of the investment.

While our journey in this book might be coming to a close, your journey into real estate success is just beginning. Take what you've learned here, implement, experiment, network with others in your space who are doing well and keep running toward your dream.

Before we part ways, let me share a full glossary of real estate terminology you need to know as well as resources that will help you with your continued education.

Full Glossary:

Accrued Interest

Accumulated interest earned or due but not yet paid

Acre

A measure of land equaling 43,560 square feet.

Adjusted Cost Basis

For accounting purposes, this is the original cost plus improvements minus depreciation or cost recovery taken.

After-Tax Cash Flow

Effective gross income minus operating expenses and debt service plus or minus any tax savings or liability.

Agency

A relationship of trust whereby one part (the principal), entrusts another party (the agent) to act in their behalf and to represent them in doing business with other parties.

Alligator

A property that has a negative cash flow.

All-Inclusive Trust Deed (AITD)

The borrower obtains a new mortgage, which is structured to include the old mortgage. The borrower makes payments on the new mortgage directly to the lender, who makes payments on the old first mortgage.

Amortization

A method of gradually paying off principal on a mortgage. Each payment reduced (amortizes) the original amount.

Amortized loan

A loan in which the principal, as well as the interest, is payable in monthly or other periodic installments over the term of the loan.

Administrator

A party appointed by a court to administer the estate of a person who has died without leaving a will.

Annuity

A payment of equal installments paid periodically for a given number of periods.

Appraisal

An estimation of the value of real property at the present time or past date, never future. Any of the three methods are used where applicable.

a. Cost approach

b. Income approach.

c. Market data approach.

Appraiser

A disinterested party who evaluates a property and determines its value.

Appreciation

A property's growth in value.

Arrears

The payment of money after the fact. Interest and taxes paid in arrears would represent money paid for a period gone by.

Asking Price

This is the price an appraiser has determined for a property and the price for which it is on the market.

Assessed Value

This is the value as determined by the local tax assessor's office to levy local taxes.

Assessment

This is the value set on a property by the local government for the purpose of real estate taxes.

Asset

This is any possession of value that an individual owns which may be used for payment of a debt.

Assign

To transfer one's rights in a bond, lease, mortgage, or other legal instruments to another person.

Assuming Mortgage

This is the taking of title to a property by a buyer, whereby he or she assumes payment of note or bond secured by a mortgage against the property.

Balance Sheet

This is a financial statement showing assets, liabilities, and net worth.

Balloon Payment

A large financial payment due on a note, usually after partial amortization of the debt through installment payments.

Bankruptcy

Proceedings against a debtor, who has been declared legally insolvent, to distribute the debtor's property among the creditors.

Binder

This is a small deposit of money paid with a temporary agreement to purchase property under specified terms.

Bird Dog

A person who is on the lookout for properties that are for sale.

Blanket Mortgage

One mortgage that covers several different parcels of real property.

Blended Interest Rate

This is the interest rate resulting from half the difference of the interest rate initially written for the mortgage and the current market rate of interest.

Book Value

The value of property carried on a company's books. It is usually the cost minus depreciation or cost recovery plus capital additions.

Bond

This is the evidence of a personal debt, which is secured by a mortgage on real estate.

Broker

This is a state licensed agent who represents buyers and sellers in real estate proceedings.

Brokers price opinion

This is the opinion of a Real Estate Broker as to the value of a property (like a "lite" appraisal) often abbreviated as BPO.

Capital

This is the money used for investment purposes.

Capital Gains

This is the profit realized above the adjusted cost basis on the sale of a property.

Cash Flow

This is the effective gross income minus operating expenses and debt service.

Caveat Emptor

This is Latin for "let the buyer beware." The buyer must inspect the goods or property and purchase at their own risk.

Chattel

This is personal property.

Chattel Mortgage

A mortgage on a personal property.

Closing

This is the procedure whereby the property title is conveyed from seller to buyer.

Collateral

Real or personal property pledged as security for repayment of a loan or debt.

Commission

This is usually a percentage of the purchase price paid to the broker or agent for services rendered.

Condemnation

This is the process by which property of a private owner is taken, with or without consent, for the public use. Fair compensation must be paid.

Condominium

Individual ownership of an apartment and an undivided interest in the common areas and facilities, which serve the multi-unit property.

Contingency

A possible event based on the happening of an uncertain future event.

Contract

An agreement between competent parties in the performance of a legal consideration, whereby each party obtains a right to what the other wants.

Contract For Deed

A contract for the sale of real property wherein the seller is obligated to provide a merchantable title after the buyer has paid for the property, usually in installments. Commonly abbreviated as CFD. Also called Land Contract (LC) or Agreement for Deed (AD).

Contract For Purchase And Sale

An agreement between buyer and seller for real property to transfer title to that property at a future time for a specific sum of money.

Conveyance

The transfer of real estate from one party to another.

Cooperative

An apartment house or similar property owned in corporate form by all the tenants. Each has stock in the corporation, which owns the building.

Covenant

Insertion of a written agreement into deeds and other documents promising performance of certain acts, or stating specific uses of real estate.

Cow

This is a term used to describe an income property with a high positive cash flow.

Creditor

The lender. The one to whom the debt is owed.

Cure Date

The last day given for bringing mortgage payments current at the beginning of the foreclosure process.

Dead Asset

This is an asset that an investor does not want (in the investor's eyes it has no value).

Debt Service

The sum of the annual principal and interest payments expressed as a percentage of the amount owed.

Deed

A legal document, which conveys real estate from seller to buyer when properly, executed.

Default

Failure to discharge a duty or meet your obligation.

Deficiency Judgment

A judgment rendered in court for the difference in the amount realized at a foreclosure sale and the amount owed by the mortgagor, if the foreclosure sale fails to liquidate or satisfy the debt entirely.

Depreciation

This is the decline in property value due to obsolescence, natural wear, age, or any other condition.

Discount

This is the percentage of the original balance of the loan that is charged the borrower. Sometimes referred to as points. It's also the difference between the selling price of a mortgage and the amount due.

Discounting A Note

This is the process of offering a promissory note for less than its face value to enhance its marketability.

Distressed property

This is a bargain property that is substantially below its present or projected renovated value.

Duplex

This is a two family home where the units share a common divider and are situated either side by side or up and down.

Earnest Money

This is a deposit of money given by a party to bind the contract usually credited toward the sales price.

Effective Gross Income

This is the difference between the total gross income and vacancy allowance.

Effective Interest

This is the interest rate the borrower actually pays as opposed to the nominal interest rate. The effective interest rate is made higher than the nominal rate by addition of points or discounting a loan.

Eminent Domain

This is the power of the government to take private property for public use in return for fair compensation. This power is exercised through condemnation.

Encroachment

An obstruction or building, which intrudes upon or trespasses upon the property of another.

Encumbrance

This is anything that mars title to a property such as a mechanic's liens, lien for back taxes, an unpaid mortgage, judgment, etc.

Equity

This is the value of a property minus the debts or liens against it. It increases in margin over the years as the mortgage is paid off.

Escape clause

A clause added to the contract that allows either party the option of exiting the contract. Both parties are no longer bound by any contractual obligations.

Escrow

Funds held by a third party to be released when certain conditions are in a contract are fulfilled.

Estate

Ownership interest in real property.

Estate by the entireties

Ownership by husband and wife with the right of survivorship.

Estoppel Letter

A letter certifying the exact balance of a mortgage or another loan at a given time.

Exchange

This is the exchanging or trading of a business property you own for another trade or business property that is like it. No taxes are due in such an exchange under a given set of circumstances.

Exculpatory clause

This is a clause in a contract relieving one of the parties of personal responsibility or liability.

Expenses

The cost of maintenance, repairs, and rental costs that are deducted from a property's gross income.

Extension Clause

This is a clause contained within some lease option contracts that provides for the terms under which the contract may be extended.

Face Value

This is in reference to a note. The face value is the full amount for which the note has been written.

Fair Market Value

This is the appraised value of a property as compared with other property values on the market.

Flipping

The turnover of a property. This is where an investor buys a property to sell it for a profit immediately.

Fiduciary

An agent in the position of confidence to his principal. It's also a relationship of trust and confidence imposed by law.

Financial Analysis

This is an investor's determination of the value of a property according to their specific needs.

Financial Leverage

This is the use of other people's money for investment purposes.

Financing

This is the way in which an investor obtains the capital with which to purchase a property.

First Deed Of Trust

This is a deed of trust recorded first. Equivalent to a first mortgage.

Forced Sale

This is the sale of a property used as security for a loan to repay the creditor, or others, in the event of default on the loan.

Foreclosure

A legal procedure where the lending institution or agency sells the property because the borrower is in default of the payment terms of the mortgage.

General Partnership

This is a form of business where two or more individuals enter into an agreement to conduct business. Profits and losses are shared in a predetermined fashion, and all partners are jointly and severally liable for debts of the general partnership.

Grace Period

Additional time granted to perform an act or make a payment before default.

Grandfather clause

Properties that do not conform to current ordinances, regulations or codes, but are allowed to continue to be occupied because the properties predate the institution of the ordinances, codes, and regulations.

Grantee

This is a person or entity that is receiving interests or rights of real estate. For example, a buyer.

Grantor

This is a person or entity that conveys their interests or rights in real estate. For example, a seller.

Gross Income

This is the total income from a property before the deduction of expenses.

Gross Income Multiplier

This is the number which when multiplied times the gross number, would give an indication of property value. It is strictly a guide.

Homestead Exemption

This is protection extended by the law preventing the forced sale of an owner-occupied dwelling by certain creditors.

Homestead Tax Exemption

This is the credit against taxes given in some states to individuals who own and occupy a dwelling and to certain other individuals including disabled veterans, those over 65 years old, widowed, or handicapped.

Installment Loan

This is a loan that must be repaid in no less than two payments. A loan of six months or greater is preferable when establishing credit.

Installment Note

This is a note, which specifies how mortgage payments will be made, when they will be due and for what amount.

Installment Sale

This is a sale whereby (for income tax purposes) it is not taxed totally in the first year of the sale. For this to be valid, there must be a minimum of two installment payments over two tax years.

Instrument

A written legal document delineating the rights of the parties.

Interest Rate

An amount a borrower must repay in addition to the full amount of the loan.

Intestate

An individual who has dies without leaving a valid will.

Involuntary lien

A lien, like real property tax liens, which are recorded against the property without the consent of the owner.

Instant Equity

The difference between the property's value and what you paid for it.

Joint Tenancy

Ownership of real estate by two or more persons, each of whom has an undivided interest with the right of survivorship.

Joint Venture

An arrangement where two or more individuals or corporations join together on a single project as partners.

Jointly and Severally

This is a legal term indicating that two parties have entered into a contract and the two parties are not only liable together but individually as well.

Judgment

This is the verdict of a court on a matter presented to it. A money judgment dictates that a party must make payments to another to settle a claim.

Junior Lien

This is a mortgage or other encumbrance with a secondary interest. A lien junior to another mortgage or lien.

Lease

A contractual agreement between the owner and the tenant, which allows the tenant the use and occupancy of the property for a specified period of time. A lease is an encumbrance against a title and gives the tenant an actual interest in the property for years.

Lease Option

This is an agreement between two parties where the party that owns the property extends the right to purchase the property at a future date. The second party lives in the property until the lease option expires. Commonly abbreviated as LO or L/O.

Leasehold

The estate or interest held by the lessee in the property of another.

Legal Description

This is the means to identify the exact boundaries of a property. A surveyor will use the recorded plat method, metes, and bounds method or the government survey method to describe a real property.

Lessee

An individual who contracts to hold occupancy rights in the real estate property of another.

Letter Of Credit

This is a letter usually from a financial institution, guaranteeing a debt incurred by a third party.

Letter of Intent

This is a letter stating a buyer's intent to make an offer to acquire a specific property. It is not a binding contract.

Leverage

This implies obtaining a higher return on borrowed money than the cost of borrowing it. It's a situation where the smallest amount of cash is invested in obtaining the best yield, percentage-wise.

Lien

This is a claim lodged against real estate to effect repayment of indebtedness. For example, a mechanic's lien, where the contractor records his or her lien for work done and not paid for.

Limited Partnership

This is a partnership composed of a limited partner and a general partner. The limited partner contributes capital but is not liable for any debts of the partnership, nor can they manage or control the partnership.

Listing

This is an agreement whereby the owner of a property gives a real estate agent the right to handle the sale, lease of property and to receive a commission for this service.

Marketable Title

A title free and clear of liens and encumbrances that might be objectionable.

Market Value

This is the highest price for a property that a buyer is willing to pay and the lowest prices that a seller agrees to accept.

Mechanics Lien

A lien existing in favor of mechanics, suppliers or other persons who have supplied materials or performed work in connection with the construction or rehabilitation of a building.

Mete

Measures such as inches, yards, miles or feet.

Metes And Bounds

A description of the boundary lines of land, setting forth the boundary lines within their terminal points and angles.

Moratorium Of Interest

A time during the term of a loan wherein no payment of interest due is made.

Mortgage

This is a legal document that conveys title to real estate as collateral for the payment of a debt.

Mortgagee

The lender of money who holds a mortgage on a property as security for repayment of the loan.

Mortgagor

The borrower of money who gives a mortgage on a property as collateral for repayment of the loan.

Mortgage Commitment

This is a formal notice from a lending institution stating the amount it will lend for the purchase of the property.

Multiple Listing Service

This is a multi-realty service whereby members of the local Board of Realtors exchange their listings.

Negative Cash Flow

This is a property that costs you money instead of making your monthly income.

Net Income Approach

This is a technique used to evaluate larger properties to determine their value. It is done by calculating the net income they produce.

Net Listing

A price under which an owner will not sell the property. The broker is entitled to the excess over the net listing as his commission.

Net Net Net (Triple Net Lease)

An agreement, which specifies that the tenant pays real estate taxes, insurance and all maintenance, costs of the property.

Net Operating Income (NOI)

This is the gross income minus any operating expenses. Debt service is not deducted as an expense and therefore not included here.

435

Net Spendable Income

This is the amount remaining after expenses and debt service and any taxes due have been deducted from the gross income.

No Doc Loan

This is a loan where the borrower is not required to present any documentation to secure a loan.

Non-Owner Occupant (NOO)

This is a property where the owner does not live. Generally refers to rental property.

Note

This is the legal evidence of debt.

Option

An instrument giving the right to a party to lease or purchase the property over a specified time period for detailed consideration. It is binding for the optionor but not the optionee.

Optionee

The person who has the legal right to purchase or not purchase a specific property in the future.

Optionor

The seller of a property who extends an option to someone else. If the optionee exercises the option, this person is legally bound by the contractual obligations. If the option is not exercised, then the optionor is released from any responsibilities.

Owners Of Record

This is a record of all the owners that are listed on a deed. It is recorded in the county courthouse.

Package Mortgage

This is a mortgage, which in addition to encumbering real property also includes personal property such as a dishwasher, refrigerator or oven.

Partnership

Two or more people associated for the purpose of carrying on business activities.

Pay Down

This is the amount of principal on a loan retired through payments at a given time.

Personal Property

All property besides real property.

Plat Book

A public record containing maps of land showing the division of such land into streets, blocks and lots. It also includes measurements of individual parcels.

Points

An originating fee or a percentage based on the amount of mortgage money advanced, to be paid by the seller.

Positive Cash Flow

This is when rental and other income exceeds all of the costs and expenses of ownership.

Preliminary Title Search

This is the first review of all previously recorded documents regarding a specific property, to make sure that property may be sold.

Premium

This is an additional sum of money paid as an incentive for someone to do something.

Prepayment Clause

This is a clause in a mortgage giving the mortgagor the privilege of paying off the mortgage before its due date.

Principal

This is the sum of money used as funds for the investment.

Promissory Note

This is usually a note given to the seller by the buyer, which promises to pay back principal to the seller. It also states the interest rate and the timeframe for payback.

Pro Forma Statement

This is a financial statement based on anticipated, not actual income and expenses.

Pro Rata

Buyers and sellers portion of prepaid or unpaid expenses such as real estate taxes.

Purchase Money Mortgage

These are funds advanced in the form of a mortgage by the owner of the real estate to the buyer for the purpose of buying their property.

Quit Claim Deed

A deed transferring whatever interest in the property that the grantor may have and is commonly used to clear title.

Real Property

Land, and generally any improvements added to the land.

Real Estate Owned (R.E.O)

These are properties that financial institutions have repossessed as a result of default on a mortgage and which these institutions (such as banks), are willing to sell.

Recording

The act of entering in the public record any instrument affecting title to real property.

Release Clause

A statement in a blanket mortgage that allows a specifically described parcel to be released from under the blanket lien after a sum of money is paid, or a period is up.

Reproduction Cost Analysis

This is a technique used to evaluate a property by estimating the cost of building the same or similar structure, adding the cost of land and subtracting an allowance for wear and tear.

Sandwich Lease

While having the option to buy a property, the investor subleases it to gain positive cash flow.

Security Deposit

This is the amount of money paid by a tenant before moving into the premises to cover any damage incurred while living there, or to protect the landlord in the event that the tenant leaves without being current on rent payments. If the tenant is current and the unit only has a reasonable amount of wear and teat, then the deposit is generally refunded.

Subject To

This is a term that means "buying a property with an encumbrance in place." In Real Estate Investing, it is generally a method of buying a property without getting new financing. Buying a house with a mortgage in place. Commonly abbreviated as Sub2, Sub-2, Sub To and Sub-To.

Survey

This is a map prepared by land engineers or surveyors indicating the location and boundaries of the property described in the title.

Tax Certificates

These are bonds sold to recoup unpaid property taxes by the country in which the property is located. When the property is auctioned, the certificate holders may either use the certificates as money to bid on the property or redeem them for face value plus interest.

Tax Sale

The sale of a property because of a delinquency in the payment of taxes.

Tenant

A person having the temporary use and occupancy of real property owned by another.

Terms

The exact way a property will be purchased.

Testate

An individual who dies leaving a valid will

Tile

A legal document certifying the right of ownership or property.

Title Insurance

Insurance issues by a guarantee company protecting the property owner against any flaws in the title that might affect ownership or potential losses.

Title Insurance Company

A business that reports on the status for the title on a specific property and whether or not it has any liens against it. After this title search is completed, the company will issue a deed to be signed by all the owners of the property, which should be notarized and recorded in the public records.

Title Search

This involves the investigation of title records; history of previous ownership to ascertain if liens, encumbrances or other outstanding claims exist that may prevent legal conveyance of title.

Township

This is a unit of measure used in the government survey method of land description equal to 36 sections, which is 36 square miles.

Unilateral Contract

This is a contract in which one party is bound by another to do something. If the second party chooses to exercise the contract, the first party must perform any contractual obligations that the party may have. If the second party chooses not to exercise the contract, the first party is released from any contractual obligations.

Unsecured Line Of Credit

This is a credit history developed by an individual who borrows small amounts of money, which do not require collateral.

Usury

This is a rate of interest on a loan, which is greater than the law allows.

Vacancy Rate

This is an estimate of the amount of time the rental property will be vacant multiplied by the rental rate of the unit(s). The amount is used in estimating the investor's value of an income property.

Violation

An act, deed or creation of a condition that violates the law in the use of the property.

Warrant

To guarantee something to be as represented.

Win-Win

A solution to both seller and buyer needs.

Wraparound Mortgage

A mortgage held by the seller-mortgagee. The buyer-mortgagee pays the seller-mortgagee the debt service on the wraparound mortgage, and the seller-mortgagee continues to pay the debt service on the underlying or original mortgage.

Zone

An area designated by the authorities for a specific use, subject to certain restrictions.

For more resources on real estate here are some recommendations.

1. Bigger Pockets - https://www.biggerpockets.com

2. National Real Estate Investment Group (Investing Education) - https://www.nreigrp.com/blog/

www.ingramcontent.com/pod-product-compliance
Lightning Source LLC
Chambersburg PA
CBHW081437190326
41458CB00020B/6225